Preface

Maths Cloud Ltd was founded by a number of Maths teachers with [...]
resources and content to support and aid teachers in teaching Math [...]
and across the world.

The team initially developed an online teaching platform which was launched in 2015. This has received great reviews and feedback from teachers.

It has seen significant growth and usage since it's launch and is now used across the UK and internationally.

Due to repeated requests from students wishing for supportive documents and resources to our teaching platform, we launched **maths-school**, which is a suite of content to support students outside the classroom.

This maths-school skills workbook, and our other workbooks, have been specifically designed and developed to support students in practising the skills taught within the classroom.

All our skills workbooks include examples, exam style questions and a complete set of answers.

We continue to work hard to develop and enhance our offering, so please ensure that you follow us on Facebook and take advantage of our detailed explanations of the topics on our website Maths-School.co.uk

This is the 1st workbook in a series of 3 workbooks aimed towards Edexcel iGCSE. We strongly recommend that you complete this workbook, before moving onto our 2nd workbook (Grades 4 to 5)

Contents

Contents

Contents

Place value

A digits value depends on where it sits in a number. The numbers positioned around the decimal point have a "place value" as shown →

Each digit in its given place has a specific "value".

In this example : The 6 represents six hundred and the 3 represents thirty.

Thousands	Hundreds	Tens	Units	Tenths	Hundredths	Thousandths
5 , 6	3	4 . 9	2	1		

Examples

Identify the value of the digit underlined:

a) 5,3<u>2</u>1   **Three hundred**

b) 2<u>6</u>,321   **Six thousand**

c) 4<u>1</u>0,321   **Ten thousand**

d) 8<u>6</u>,410,321   **Six million**

Practice questions:

Identify the value of the underlined digits:

a) 4<u>5</u>2

b) <u>8</u>33

c) <u>9</u>,174

d) <u>7</u>0,912

e) 2<u>3</u>,040

f) <u>5</u>67,073

g) 64<u>3</u>,541

h) <u>7</u>,432,852

Examples

Identify the value of the digit underlined:

a) 321.1<u>5</u>3   **Five hundredths**

b) 6.<u>2</u>11   **Two tenths**

c) 55.10<u>6</u>   **Six thousandths**

d) 8.4156<u>2</u>   **Two hundred thousandths**

Practice questions:

Identify the value of the underlined digits:

i) 2.<u>5</u>2

j) 1.<u>8</u>33

k) 4.2<u>9</u>

l) 1.0<u>8</u>2

m) 203.<u>1</u>46

n) 347.0<u>7</u>01

o) 542.21<u>5</u>

p) 437,642.2<u>1</u>

Exam question

2   3   5   6   8

Using the set of cards shown :

a) Write down the value of the digit 5 in the number shown.

b) What is the largest number you can make using all five cards?

c) What is the largest multiple of 5 that you can make using all five cards?

(3)

Numbers in and from words

When looking at numbers, you need to read them in groups of three.

$$8\ 4\ 5\ ,\ 6\ 3\ 4\ ,\ 9\ 2\ 1$$

Millions   Thousands

This number is read as:

Eight hundred and forty five <u>million</u>, 6 hundred and thirty four <u>thousand</u>, nine hundred and twenty one

Examples

a) Write in words: 5,462   **Five thousand, four hundred and sixty two**

b) Write in words: 203,720   **Two hundred and three thousand, seven hundred and twenty**

c) Write in words: 1,013,005   **One million, thirteen thousand and five**

Practice questions:

Write these numbers in words:

a) 452

b) 833

c) 9,174

d) 7,062

e) 23,940

f) 56,702

g) 643,541

h) 7,432,852

Examples

Write in figures:

a) Twenty five thousand, four hundred and sixty two   **25,462**

b) Two hundred & three thousand, seven hundred and twenty   **203,720**

c) Six million, three thousand, five hundred and fourteen   **6,003,514**

Practice questions:

Write these words in figures:

i) Eight hundred and sixty three

j) Twenty nine thousand, two hundred and eighteen

k) Four hundred and eleven thousand and twenty five

l) Six million, fourteen thousand, two hundred and twelve

m) Eighteen million, ninety thousand and twenty four

Exam question

a) Write 18,500 in words.

b) Write seven thousand, one hundred and seventeen in figures.

(2)

Ordering numbers

To order numbers you must compare the highest place values in the numbers from left to right, if they are the same, then you look at the next place value, and so on.

Example

Order the numbers in descending order (largest to smallest): **325 2462 231 1325 363**

Identify which numbers have the highest place values: 2462 and 1325

Then 231 , 363 and 325. Since 363 and 325 are both 3 hundreds, we look at the next digit 363 and 325, so next is 365, then 325 and finally 231.

2462, 1325, 363, 325 and 231

Practice questions:

Write these numbers in descending order:

a) 34, 24, 41, 14, 4

b) 523, 612, 62, 762, 712

c) 432, 653, 334, 423, 42

d) 314, 341, 353, 531,

e) 2423, 2621, 2432, 258

f) 871, 781, 873, 789

Example

Order the numbers in ascending order (smallest to largest): **1.585 3.631 3.25 0.246 2.381**

Identify which number has the smallest of the units place value: 0.246, then 1.585, then 2.381

Since 3.631 and 3.25 are both 3, we look at the next digit 3.631 and 3.25, so 3.25 is smaller than 3.631.

0.246, 1.585, 2.381, 3.25, 3.631

Practice questions:

Write these numbers in ascending order:

g) 0.4, 0.14, 0.41, 1.4

h) 0.23, 0.12, 0.26, 0.76

i) 1.4, 1.14, 0.41, 4.1, 4

j) 0.315, 0.0316, 0.3, 0.04

k) 0.351, 0.531, 0.5, 0.35

l) 8.71, 0.781, 8.73, 78.9

Exam question: The table shows the total number of pets owned within a council district.

Cat	Parrot	Dog	Rabbit	Snake
23,452	8,642	24,021	8,462	898

a) Put the pets in order of popularity, starting with least popular.

.... (1)

b) Find the difference in pets between the most and 2nd least popular pets.

(1)

3

Ordering negative numbers

To order numbers you must compare the highest place values of the numbers from left to right. If they are the same, then you look at the next place value, and so continue on. With negative numbers, the higher the absolute value, the smaller the actual value. For example: - 7 is smaller than -2.

Example
Order the numbers in descending order: **1   5   -2   -8   0   12   -11**
Identify which is the largest positive number, then work your way down to zero: 12, 5, 1 , 0
Now you look at negative numbers and work your way back up the absolute value: -2, -8, - 11

12, 5, 1 , 0, -2, -8, - 11

Practice questions:
Write these numbers in descending order:

a) -4, -2, 14, -10, 5

b) -13, 12, 11, -10, 9, -8

c) 53, -34, -42, 42, 0, 6

d) -14, 14, -1, 1, 7, -9

e) -423, -621, -432, 42

f) 71, -81, 18, -789, 790

Example
Order the numbers in ascending order: **3   16   -12   -8   8   15   -11**
Identify which is the largest negative value, then work your way down to zero, so -12, -11, -8
Now you look at positive numbers and work your way upwards, so 3, 8, 15, 16

-12, -11, -8, 3, 8, 15, 16

Practice questions:
Write these numbers in ascending order:

g) -5, -3, 3, -4, 2

h) -12, 13, 14, -15, 16, -17

i) 35, -32, -41, 24, 0, -8

j) 4, -4, -3, -18, 17, -19

k) -423, 62, -432, 421, 5

l) -71, 16, -18, -79, 80

Exam question: The table shows the outside temperatures of cities in January.

Leeds	Moscow	Sydney	Tokyo	Calgary	Detroit
-1°C	-6°C	25°C	10°C	-8°C	-4°C

a) Put the cities in order of temperature, starting with least warmest.

....   (1)

b) Find the difference in temperature between the warmest and the 2nd coldest city.

(1)

Adding numbers

When adding two numbers, we can use "columns". To do this, you **must** put one number below the other, ensuring that you line up the place values in columns (ones, tens, hundreds etc).

Example (Column addition)
Calculate: 285 + 47
Step 1: Line up the numbers.
Step 2: Always move from right to left. Add the "units" column first. 5 + 7 = 12.
        The 2 goes in the at the bottom and the 1 is carried to the tens column.
Step 3: Add the tens column (Do not forget to add any carried numbers) 8 + 4 + 1 = 13.
Step 4: Add the hundreds column (2 + 1)

```
      Hundreds
        Tens
        Units
      2  8  5
   +     4  7
      1  1
   ─────────────
      3  3  2
```

Practice questions:
Calculate:

a) 46 + 89   b) 37 + 46   c) 452 + 279   d) 842 + 379   e) 5572 + 2179   f) 1593 + 5679

Example (Column addition with decimals)
Calculate: 6.32 + 5.8
When adding decimals, you must make sure the decimal places are lined up.
To avoid errors, it is best to fill any gaps with zero place holders.
Step 1: Line up the numbers with their respective place values.
Step 2: Fill the gaps with **zeros**.
Step 3: Add the column from the right (starting with the hundredths in this case).
Step 4: Ensure that the decimal place remains in place within your answer.

```
       Units
       Tenths
       Hundredths
      6 . 3 2
   + 5 . 8 0
     1 1
   ────────────
    1 2 . 1 2
```

Practice questions:
Calculate:

g) 3.2 + 4.9   h) 12.7+ 4.62   i) 0.38 + 2.75   j) 15.24 + 76.19   k) 0.38 + 2.75   l) 86.39 + 17.92

📋 **Exam question:** Work out the perimeter of the shape shown.

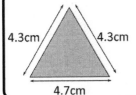

4.3cm   4.3cm

4.7cm

(2)

5

Subtracting numbers

When subtracting two numbers, we can use "columns". To do this, you **must** put the smaller number below the larger number, ensuring that you line up the place values in columns (ones, tens, hundreds etc).

Example (Column subtraction)

Calculate: 285 - 47

Step 1: Line up the numbers.

Step 2: Subtract the 1st column from the right (units), if the top number is smaller you need to exchange a number from the left. In this example, the 8 goes down to a 7, and we put 1 in front of the 5, so it is now treated as 15 (15 − 7 = 8).

Step 3: Continue with each column (7 − 4 = 3), (2 − 0 = 2).

$$
\begin{array}{r}
\text{Hundreds} \; \text{Tens} \; \text{Units} \\
2\,{}^{7}\!8\,{}^{1}5 \\
-\quad 4\;7 \\
\hline
2\,3\,8
\end{array}
$$

Practice questions:

Calculate:

a) 93 - 78

b) 450 - 231

c) 1152 – 198

d) 3542 - 2679

e) 5892 – 1098

f) 5142 - 2679

Example (Column subtraction with decimals)

Subtract 5.43 from 9.8

When subtracting decimals, you must make sure the decimal places are lined up.

To avoid errors, it is best to fill any gaps with zero place holders.

Step 1: Line up the numbers with their respective place values.

Step 2: Fill the gaps with **zeros**.

Step 3: Subtract the columns from the right (starting with the hundredths in this case).

Step 4: Ensure that the decimal place remains in place within your answer.

$$
\begin{array}{r}
\text{Units} \; \text{Tenths} \; \text{Hundredths} \\
9\,.\,{}^{7}\!8\,{}^{1}0 \\
-\;5\,.\,4\,3 \\
\hline
4\,.\,3\,7
\end{array}
$$

Practice questions:

Calculate:

g) 8.7 – 5.9

h) 12.2 – 6.5

i) 8.53 – 2.89

j) 76.52 – 14.23

k) 8.123 – 2.74

l) 76.523 – 0.98

Exam question: Christopher buys:

3 bottles of water costing £1.12 each, 1 chocolate bar costing £0.75 and 1 ham salad sandwich, costing £2.40.

How much change does he get from £10?

(2)

Multiplying numbers

When multiplying two numbers, you can set up the calculation in a number of ways.
- Like an addition problem, but you multiply the numbers instead. You would just carry any digits over to the next place value column, like you would do in column addition
- You can use the "grid method" which ensures that you don't miss out any calculations

Example (Column multiplication)

Calculate: 346 x 32

Step 1: Line up the numbers.

Step 2: Start with the 2 in 32 and multiply the top numbers by this (692).

Step 3: Now multiply the 3 in 32, but you must put a **zero** in the right column, as the 3 represents 30 .

Step 4: Add the two answers using column addition.

```
    3 4 6
     3 2
    ─────
    6 9 2
 + 1 0 3 8 0
   ─────────
   1 1 0 7 2
```

Practice questions:

Calculate:

a) 14 x 21

b) 73 x 19

c) 183 x 25

d) 245 x 17

Example (Grid method)

Calculate: 346 x 32

Step 1: Split the number into their separate place value (e.g 300, 40 and 6).

Step 2: Create a table with one number going down on the left column, and the other, along the top in a row (see diagram).

Step 3: Multiply each row & column (300 x 30, 30 x 40, 30 x 6, 2 x 300, 2 x 40, 2 x 6).

Step 4: Add all the numbers together (9000 + 1200 + 180 + 600 + 80 + 12).

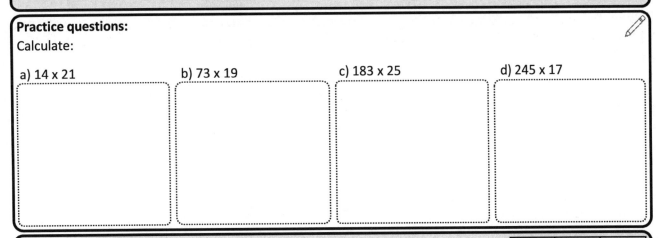

x	30	2
300	9000	600
40	1200	80
6	180	12

Toral = 11,072

Practice questions:

Calculate:

e) 531 x 12

g) 37 x 126

f) 412 x 35

h) 131 x 78

Exam question: Mr Tasker is on holiday in Scotland and is putting petrol into his car.
The petrol cost 68 pence per litre. He puts in 32 litres.
How much does the petrol he put in his car cost in **pounds**?

(2)

Multiplying and dividing by powers of 10

When multiplying by a power of 10, you move the digits to the **left** by the number of zeros.
So for example, 100 has 2 zeros so multiplying by 100 means you move the digits 2 places to the left.

When dividing by a power of 10, you move the digits to the **right** by the number of zeros.
So for example, 1000 has 3 zeros so dividing by 1000 means you move the digits 3 places to the right.

Examples

a) 62 x 10

		Th	H	T	U	.	t	h	th
				6	2	.			
Answer			6	2	0	.			

b) 0.43 x 1000

		Th	H	T	U	.	t	h	th
					0	.	4	3	
Answer			4	3	0	.			

c) 62 ÷ 10

		Th	H	T	U	.	t	h	th
				6	2	.			
Answer				6	.	2			

d) 430 ÷ 1000

		Th	H	T	U	.	t	h	th
				4	3	0	.		
Answer				0	.	4	3		

Zeros are needed for these questions to the fill unit gap.   A zero is needed for this question to the fill unit gap.

Practice questions:

Calculate:

a) 15 x 100

b) 0.5 x 1000

c) 0.54 x 10

d) 1.05 x 100

e) 0.38 x 1000

f) 37 ÷ 10

g) 842 ÷ 100

h) 380.5 ÷ 10

i) 4786 ÷ 1000

It is sometimes easier to write a power of 10 in index form, especially if the value is quite large.

E.g - 10^3 means 10 x 10 x 10 = 1000 and 10^6 means 10 x 10 x 10 x 10 x 10 x 10 or 1,000,000.

Examples

a) $62 \times 10^2 = 62 \times 100$

		Th	H	T	U	.	t	h	th
				6	2	.			
Answer	6	2	0	0	.				

b) 0.025×10^5
   0.025 x 100,000

		Th	H	T	U	.	t	h	th
					0	.	0	2	5
Answer	2	5	0	0	.				

c) $62 \div 10^2 = 62 \div 100$

		Th	H	T	U	.	t	h	th
				6	2	.			
Answer				0	.	6	2		

d) $540 \div 10^4$
   540 ÷ 10,000

		Th	H	T	U	.	t	h	th
				5	4	0	.		
Answer				0	.	0	5	4	

Zeros are needed for these questions to the fill any missing gaps.

Practice questions:

Calculate:

j) 93×10^2

k) 0.52×10^3

l) 0.021×10^5

m) 17.8×10^3

n) $8200 \div 10^4$

o) $9040 \div 10^3$

p) $1.24 \div 10^3$

q) $45 \div 10^2$

r) $4520 \div 10^5$

Exam question:

a) Find the value equal to one hundred and eight thousand divided by 100.

108   1080   10,800   108,000   1,080,000

b) Identify the number which has the same value as ten million.

10^3 10^4 10^5 10^6 10^7

c) Calculate 4.2×10^2

(3)

Dividing (short division)

When dividing, you need to put the two numbers into a "bus stop". The number being divided goes under the bus stop and the number you are dividing by goes outside.

Examples

a) What is 247 ÷ 3?

$$\begin{array}{r} 2\ 4\ 8 \\ 3\overline{\smash{)}7\ ^1\!4\ ^2\!4} \end{array}$$

Step 1: Set it out in a "bus stop".
Step 2: How many 3's go into 7? (2 remainder 1) Carry the one over to change it to 14.
Step 3: How many 3's go into 14? (4 remainder 2) Carry the two over to change it to 24.
Step 4: How many 3's go into 24? (8)

b) What is 11.68 ÷ 4?

$$\begin{array}{r} 0\ 2\ .\ 9\ 2 \\ 4\overline{\smash{)}1\ ^1\!1\ .\ ^3\!6\ 8} \end{array}$$

Step 1: Set it out in a "bus stop".
Step 2: How many 4's go into 1? (0 remainder 1) Carry the one over to change it to 11.
Step 3: How many 4's go into 11? (2 remainder 3) Carry the two over to change it to 36.
Step 4: How many 4's go into 36? (9)
Step 5: How many 4's go into 8? (2)

Practice questions:

Calculate:

a) 135 ÷ 5

b) 248 ÷ 4

c) 676 ÷ 4

d) 147 ÷ 7

e) 4.65 ÷ 5

f) 9.08 ÷ 4

g) 72.9 ÷ 9

h) 4.83 ÷ 7

i) 87.5 ÷ 7

If you need to divide by a decimal, you can manipulate the question to form an equivalent calculation, so you can still use the bus stop method effectively. Sometimes you also have to go beyond the decimal point.

Examples

a) What is 276.3 ÷ 0.3?

We can treat this like we do fractions.

e.g. $\frac{1}{2} = \frac{10}{20}$, so 276.3 ÷ 0.3 = 2763 ÷ 3

$$\begin{array}{r} 0\ 9\ 2\ 1 \\ 3\overline{\smash{)}2\ ^2\!7\ 6\ 3} \end{array}$$

Answer = 921

b) What is 123 ÷ 4?

If the steps above take you beyond the decimal place, just add some zeros to allow you to work with the any carried over remainders.

$$\begin{array}{r} 0\ 3\ 0\ .\ 7\ 5 \\ 4\overline{\smash{)}1\ ^1\!2\ 3\ .\ ^3\!0\ ^2\!0} \end{array}$$

Answer = 30.75

Practice questions:

Calculate:

j) 132 ÷ 0.5

k) 256 ÷ 0.4

l) 354 ÷ 0.3

m) 462 ÷ 5

n) 1842 ÷ 8

o) 2462 ÷ 5

Exam question: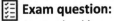

A standard barrel holds 159 litres.
A tall glass holds 0.4 litres.
If a barrel is full of wine, how many tall glasses can be **completely** filled with wine from the barrel?

(2)

Order of operations (BIDMAS)

If there are multiple operations in one calculation, BIDMAS tells us the order in which must calculate them.

Brackets   **I**ndices   **D**ivision   **M**ultiplication   **A**ddition   **S**ubtraction

Examples

a) $2 + 4 \times 5$ $= 2 + 20$ **= 22**
Multiply first

b) $12 \div (5 - 1)$ $= 12 \div 4$ **= 3**
Bracket first

c) $8 + (3 + 2)^2$ $= 8 + 5^2$ $= 8 + 25$ **= 33**
Bracket first   Indices next

d) $5 \times 4^2 \div 2$ $= 5 \times 16 \div 2$ $= 5 \times 8$ **= 40**
Indices first   Divide next

Practice questions:

Calculate:

a) $4 + 3 \times 7$

b) $24 \div (3 + 5)$

c) $4 \times (5 - 3)$

d) $2 + 4 \times 8 \times 3$

e) $6 \div 3 + 9 \times 2$

f) $4 + (6 - 2) \times 7$

g) $6 \times (2 + 1)^2$

h) $(7^2 - 9) \div 10$

Here are five number cards: $\boxed{2}$ $\boxed{3}$ $\boxed{4}$ $\boxed{5}$ $\boxed{6}$

i) Use three of the cards to complete the following. $\square + \square \times \square = \boxed{21}$

j) Use four of the cards to complete the following. $\square \times \square - \square \times \square = \boxed{9}$

Make the calculations below correct by inserting brackets in the correct place:

k) $5 \times 2 + 4 = 30$

l) $5 - 1 \times 6 + 4 = 40$

m) $2 + 6^2 - 7 = 57$

n) $4 \times 5 + 4 \times 3 = 68$

BIDMAS is sometimes referred to as BODMAS where the O stands for ORDER, but the order of operations are exactly the same. Order is the same as Indices (square roots, cube roots, powers, exponents, etc)

Exam question:

Beth says $5 - 2^2$ is 9.
Pat says $5 - 2^2$ is 1.
Who is correct? Give a reason for your answer.

(1)

ODD or EVEN: Even numbers are in the two times table, odd numbers are not.
Even numbers end in a 2, 4, 6, 8 or 0. Odd numbers end in a 1, 3, 5, 7 or 9.

Examples

Odd or Even?
a) 8   **Even** – in the two times table and ends in a 8
b) 17   **Odd** – not in the two times table and ends in a 7
c) 28465   **Odd** – It ends in a 5 so is not in the two times table

Practice questions:

Are these numbers odd or even?

a) 22

b) 37

c) 81

d) 156

e) 3,330

f) 4567

g) 26,880

h) 97,532

i) 48,843

PRIME: A prime number has only 2 Factors. 1 and itself. It must be a natural number (not negative).

Examples:

Is it Prime?

List of prime numbers : 2, 3, 5, 7, 11, 13, 17, 19, 23, 29

a) 6 **No** – 2 and 3 are also factors   b) 11 **Yes** – only 1 and 11 are factors   c) 9 **No** – 3 is also a factor

Practice questions: **HINT:** Use a calculator to find factors

Are these numbers prime?

j) 12

k) 21

l) 1

m) 17

n) 18

o) 25

p) 31

q) 49

r) 37

TRIANGULAR: Triangular Number can be arranged into a triangle as shown below
1 is the first triangular number. to get the next triangular number,
you must add 1 more than you did the time before.
1, then 1 + 2, then 1 + 2 + 3, then 1 + 2 + 3 + 4 and so on...

List of triangular numbers : 1, 3, 6, 10, 15, 21, 28, 36, 45, 55

RATIONAL / IRRATIONAL

Rational numbers can be written as a fraction where the numerator and denominator are integers.
Rational numbers are: integers, terminating decimals and recurring decimals.
Irrational numbers cannot be written as a fraction with two integers, they are endless decimals which are
not recurring (digits don't repeat).

Examples

Rational or Irrational?

a) 6 **Rational** (integer)   b) 4.73 **Rational** (it terminates)   c) 0.2451876329... **Irrational** – not repeating

Exam question:
Match up these number with
their correct classification.

The first one is done for you.

Rational	21
Prime	5
Triangular	0.5
Even	5.73257524...
Irrational	8

(2)

Multiples and lowest common multiples (LCM)

A multiple of a number is **any** number in it's times table. 20 is a multiple 5 because 20 is in the 5 times table.

Example

List the first five multiples of 4.

Following the 4 times table $1 \times 4 = 4$, $2 \times 4 = 8$, $3 \times 4 = 12$, $4 \times 4 = 16$, $5 \times 4 = 20$

The first 5 multiples of 4 are **4, 8, 12, 16 and 20**.

Practice questions:

Write the first 5 multiples of the following numbers:

a) 3

b) 5

c) 11

d) 7

e) 15

f) 16

g) 25

h) 19

i) 27

j) 34

k) 62

l) 125

The **lowest common multiple (LCM)** of two or more numbers is the smallest value that appears in both of the numbers times tables.

Example

Find the lowest common multiple of 6 and 8.

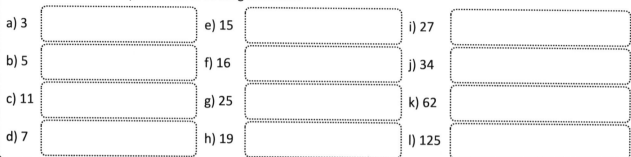

Multiples of 6: 6   12   18   (24)   30   36   Multiples of 8: 8   16   (24)   32   40   48

24 is the lowest number in both of the lists.   **Lowest common multiple (LCM) = 24**

Practice questions:

Find the lowest common multiple (LCM) of the following set of numbers:

m) 3 and 5

n) 5 and 6

o) 2 and 7

p) 4 and 17

q) 6 and 10

r) 32 and 48

s) 3, 4 and 5

t) 2,3 and 7

u) 5, 10 and 11

v) 5, 6 and 12

Exam question:

A blue light flashes every 8 seconds. A red light flashes every 5 seconds.

They both flash at the same time.

After how many seconds will they next both flash at the same time?

(2)

Factors and highest common factors (HCF)

A factor is a whole number which divides exactly into another whole number, leaving **no** remainder.
3 is a factor of 12 because you can divide 12 by 3 to get a whole number (4).

Example

List all the factors of 20.
The following numbers are all a factor of 20 : 1 and 20, 2 and 10, 4 and 5.
Factors are often paired as their product is the given number.   **Answer = 1, 2, 4, 5, 10 and 20**

FACT: Prime numbers only have 2 factors – the prime number itself and the number 1

Practice questions:

List all the factors of the following numbers:

a) 12

b) 16

c) 21

d) 15

e) 38

f) 49

g) 37

h) 50

i) 78

j) 24

k) 64

l) 84

The **highest common factor (HCF)** of two or more numbers is the largest factor of the given values which is common in those given values.

Example

Find the Highest Common Factor of 12 and 16.

Factors of 12:   1   2   3   ④   6   12   Factors of 16:   1   2   ④   8   16

4 is the largest number in both lists.   **Highest common factor (HCF) = 4**

Practice questions:

Find the highest common factor (HCF) of the following set of numbers:

m) 10 & 15

n) 14 & 21

o) 22 & 16

p) 12 & 32

q) 24 & 33

r) 60 & 90

s) 48 & 84

t) 36 & 60

u) 51 & 75

v) 54 & 63

Exam question:

Jude is thinking of a single digit integer which is a factor of 28.
The number is also 1 more than a prime number.
What number is Jude thinking of?

(2)

13

Powers, indices and roots

POWERS/INDICES : A power or index is a small number which tells you how many times you must multiply the big number (the base) by itself. 4^3 can read as 4 to the power of 3.

Examples

a) $4^3 = 4 \times 4 \times 4 = \mathbf{64}$

b) $12^2 = 12 \times 12 = \mathbf{144}$

c) $5^1 = \mathbf{5}$ (Anything to the power 1 – is itself)

d) $1^4 = 1 \times 1 \times 1 \times 1 = \mathbf{1}$

e) $2^8 = 2 \times 2 \times 2 \times 2 \times 2 \times 2 \times 2 \times 2 = \mathbf{256}$

f) $5^0 = \mathbf{1}$ (Anything to the power 0 is always 1)

HINT : "Squared" means the number is to the power of 2. "Cubed" means the number is to the power of 3.

Practice questions:

Evaluate the following:

a) 6^2

b) 2^4

c) 3^1

d) 10^3

e) 7^2

f) 101^0

g) 3^4

h) 2^6

ROOTS: Roots are the opposite/inverse of a power. The root symbol is: $\sqrt{}$

Since $4^3 = 4 \times 4 \times 4 = 64 \quad \rightarrow \quad \sqrt[3]{64} = 4$

Examples

a) $\sqrt[3]{64} = \mathbf{4}$

b) $\sqrt[3]{27} = \mathbf{3}$

c) $\sqrt[5]{32} = \mathbf{2}$

d) $\sqrt[2]{64} = \mathbf{8}$

e) $\sqrt[2]{169} = \mathbf{13}$

f) $\sqrt[4]{16} = \mathbf{2}$

HINT : A $\sqrt{}$ symbol with no number is regularly used and always means the square root $\sqrt[2]{}$.

Practice questions:

Calculate the following:

i) $\sqrt[3]{8}$

j) $\sqrt[3]{125}$

k) $\sqrt{100}$

l) $\sqrt{121}$

m) $\sqrt[3]{1000}$

n) $\sqrt[5]{1}$

o) $\sqrt{25}$

p) $\sqrt{49}$

Index form: When $4 \times 4 \times 4$ is written as 4^3, this is called index form, and will only work if the "base" numbers are the same. E.g. $4 \times 4 \times 4 \times 3 \times 3$ is written as $4^3 \times 3^2$ in index form as the bases are different.

Examples

a) 2 x 2 x 2 in index form = 2^3

b) 5 x 5 x 5 x 5 in index form = 5^4

c) 7 x 7 in index form = 7^2

d) 3 x 3 x 3 x 3 x 3 x 3 in index form = 3^6

Exam question:

Evaluate the following:

a) $5^3 - \sqrt{100}$

b) $\sqrt{(4^2 + 3^2)}$

(2)

Identifying types of numbers

You will often be asked to pick types of numbers from a list.

Example   2 4 6 8 10 11

From the numbers above pick the:
a) Odd number   **11**
b) Prime number   **2 (only two factors)**
c) Square number   **4 (2 x 2)**
d) Cube number   **8 (2 x 2 x 2)**
e) Factor of 14   **2 (2 x 7 = 14)**
f) Multiple of 5   **10 (5, 10, 15...)**

Practice questions:

From the following numbers pick the: **5 9 10 18 20 27**

a) Odd numbers
b) Even numbers
c) Square numbers
d) Cube numbers

e) Factors of 40
f) Multiples of 9
g) Prime numbers
h) Triangular numbers

15 16 17 19 21 125

i) Odd numbers
j) Even numbers
k) Square numbers
l) Cube numbers

m) Factors of 105
n) Multiples of 7
o) Prime numbers
p) Triangular numbers

1 6 12 23 36 64 78

q) Odd numbers
r) Even numbers
s) Square numbers
t) Cube numbers

u) Factors of 72
v) Multiples of 13
w) Prime numbers
x) Triangular numbers

Exam question:

Here is a list of numbers:

          45 48 53 56 70 77 81

From the list of numbers:
a) Write down an odd number

b) Write down a multiple of 7

c) Write down a square number

(3)

Venn diagrams

Venn diagrams are used to sort data into groups, and these groups are represented by circles.
The area where circles overlap represent where information meets more than one groups' criteria.

Example

Put these numbers into the Venn Diagram:
10, 3, 15, 8, 5, 7, 20

- 5, 10, 15 and 20 go in the circle for 5x table
- 3, 5, 7 and 15 go in the circle for odd
- Since 5 and 15 fall into both categories, they go into the overlap.
- 8 does not sit into any category, so goes outside the circles

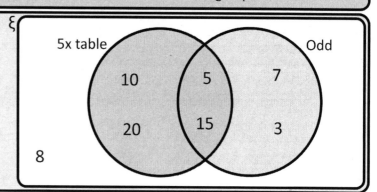

Practice questions:

Complete the Venn diagrams with the values given:

a) 9, 12, 21, 16, 7, 30, 6, 15, 8

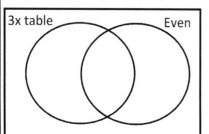

b) 5, 6, 10, 12, 15, 20, 24, 28, 30

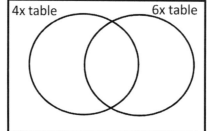

c) 3, 4, 5, 7, 9, 11, 14, 17, 21

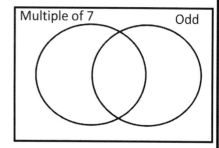

d) 1, 2, 3, 4, 6, 8, 9, 10, 12, 16

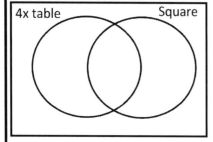

e) 1, 2, 3, 4, 5, 6, 7, 8, 9, 10

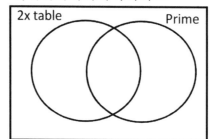

f) 1, 2, 3, 4, 5, 6, 7, 8, 9, 10

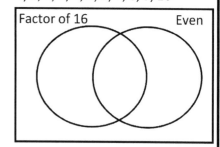

g) 2, 4, 5, 6, 8, 9, 10, 11, 12, 15

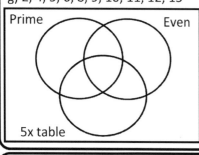

h) 1, 2, 4, 6, 8, 9, 12, 16, 27

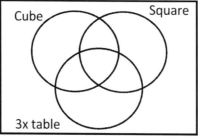

i) 1, 2, 3, 4, 5, 6, 7, 8, 9, 10

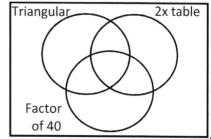

Exam question:

a) Place the numbers 1 to 15 into the Venn diagram.

b) Hence or otherwise, determine the probability of randomly choosing a value from the numbers 1 to 15, which would be an even factor of 30.

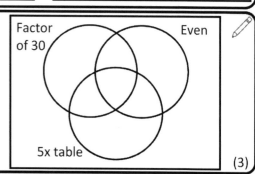

(3)

16

Equivalent fractions and simplifying fractions

You need to ensure that if a calculation has a fraction as a solution, you leave it in its simplest form.
To simplify fractions you need to find the value of the highest common factor that goes into both the numerator and the denominator of the resulting fraction.
Fractions can be simplified in stages if the highest common factor is not identified in the first instance.

Example – simplifying fractions

a) Simplify $\frac{12}{18}$

Step 1: Find a factor of both 12 and 18. e.g. 2
Step 2: Divide the numerator and denominator by this factor

$$\frac{12}{18} = \frac{12 \div 2}{18 \div 2} = \frac{6}{9}$$

Step 3: Check to see if it can be simplified again by another factor

$$= \frac{6 \div 3}{9 \div 3} = \frac{2}{3}$$

Answer $= \frac{2}{3}$

Practice questions:

Simplify the following fractions:

a) $\frac{6}{12}$

b) $\frac{5}{20}$

c) $\frac{6}{18}$

d) $\frac{12}{28}$

e) $\frac{40}{60}$

f) $\frac{18}{27}$

g) $\frac{12}{42}$

h) $\frac{14}{32}$

i) $\frac{48}{72}$

j) $\frac{63}{84}$

k) $\frac{54}{144}$

l) $\frac{84}{168}$

Equivalent fractions are the same size. Whatever you multiply or divide the numerator by, you must also do the same to the denominator for the fraction to be equivalent (same size).

Example

a) Find the missing value $\frac{3}{10} = \frac{\square}{70}$

The denominator has been multiplied by 7
We must also multiply the numerator by 7 for it to be equivalent (3 x 7 = 21)

Answer = 21

Practice questions:

Find the values of the missing letters to make the fractions equivalent:

m) $\frac{5}{6} = \frac{a}{24}$ $a =$

n) $\frac{5}{9} = \frac{b}{27}$ $b =$

o) $\frac{7}{12} = \frac{c}{36}$ $c =$

p) $\frac{8}{14} = \frac{d}{42}$ $d =$

q) $\frac{6}{e} = \frac{48}{64}$ $e =$

r) $\frac{6}{9} = \frac{f}{72}$ $f =$

s) $\frac{5}{6} = \frac{g}{108}$ $g =$

t) $\frac{5}{8} = \frac{75}{h}$ $h =$

u) $\frac{4}{i} = \frac{76}{171}$ $i =$

Exam question:

How many squares need to be shaded in the following diagram to make the amount shaded equivalent to:

a) $\frac{2}{5}$

b) $\frac{11}{15}$

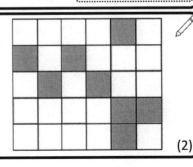

(2)

Converting mixed numbers and improper fractions

An improper fraction has a bigger numerator than denominator (top heavy).
To convert an improper fraction to a mixed number you need to see how many times the denominator goes into the numerator and find the remainder. The denominator stays the same.

Example:

a) Write $\frac{13}{5}$ as a mixed number

$2\frac{3}{5}$

5 goes into 13: 2 times with 3 left over.

b) Write $\frac{22}{3}$ as a mixed number

$7\frac{1}{3}$

3 goes into 22: 7 times with 1 left over.

Practice questions:

Write as a mixed number:

a) $\frac{8}{5}$

b) $\frac{10}{3}$

c) $\frac{17}{5}$

d) $\frac{21}{4}$

e) $\frac{19}{2}$

f) $\frac{23}{6}$

g) $\frac{29}{7}$

h) $\frac{33}{5}$

i) $\frac{47}{8}$

j) $\frac{63}{4}$

k) $\frac{95}{8}$

l) $\frac{82}{3}$

m) $\frac{27}{10}$

n) $\frac{67}{5}$

o) $\frac{82}{7}$

p) $\frac{95}{6}$

To convert a mixed number to an improper fraction you multiply the whole number by the denominator, and then add the numerator. This gives you the numerator of the improper fraction. The denominator stays the same as the original mixed number.

Example:

a) Write $4\frac{2}{3}$ as an improper fraction

$\frac{14}{3}$

4 x 3 + 2 = 14 (numerator)

b) Write $3\frac{4}{7}$ as an improper fraction

$\frac{25}{7}$

3 x 7 + 4 = 25 (numerator)

Practice questions:

Write as an improper fraction:

a) $2\frac{1}{4}$

b) $3\frac{2}{3}$

c) $6\frac{1}{2}$

d) $4\frac{3}{5}$

e) $5\frac{3}{4}$

f) $5\frac{2}{7}$

g) $8\frac{5}{6}$

h) $9\frac{3}{4}$

i) $7\frac{6}{7}$

j) $5\frac{2}{9}$

k) $9\frac{7}{8}$

l) $8\frac{4}{7}$

m) $6\frac{6}{7}$

n) $4\frac{7}{11}$

o) $3\frac{5}{12}$

p) $12\frac{3}{4}$

Exam question:

Write as a mixed number in its simplest form:

a) 2.5

b) 6.75

c) 3.4

(3)

Fractions of quantities

To calculate a fraction of an amount or quantity, you divide the amount by the denominator of the fraction and multiply that answer by the numerator.

Examples

a) Calculate $\frac{1}{3}$ of £21

$21 \div 3 \times 1 = \textbf{£7}$

b) Calculate $\frac{3}{5}$ of £45

$45 \div 5 \times 3 = \textbf{£27}$

c) Calculate $\frac{2}{9}$ of 54g

$54 \div 9 \times 2 = \textbf{12g}$

Practice questions:

Calculate:

a) $\frac{1}{2}$ of £12

b) $\frac{1}{5}$ of £30

c) $\frac{2}{3}$ of £36

d) $\frac{5}{6}$ of £42

e) $\frac{4}{9}$ of £36

f) $\frac{3}{8}$ of £64

g) $\frac{7}{12}$ of £60

h) $\frac{3}{4}$ of £700

To write one number as a fraction of another, you must put the number you want as the numerator, and the total that its out of as the denominator. Always check to see if it simplifies.

Examples

a) Write 24 out of 50 as a fraction

24 out of 50 = $\frac{24}{50}$ Simplify = $\frac{12}{25}$

b) What fraction of the shape is **not** shaded?

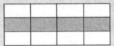

8 out of 12 = $\frac{8}{12}$ Simplify = $\frac{2}{3}$

Practice questions:

Write the fraction of the shape that is shaded in its simplest form.

i)   j)   k)

l)   m)   n)

Write the following numbers as a fraction of the other (in their simplest forms).

o) 28 out of 32

p) 14 out of 35

q) 48 out of 60

r) 48 out of 84

s) 44 out of 72

t) 8 out of 52

u) 72cm out of 4.68m

v) 36p out of £2.12

w) 8 hrs out of 5 days

Exam question:

Matt, Mark, Luke and John share £240 between them.

Matt has £55 of the money, Mark has £35, Luke has 3/8 of the money,

What fraction of the money does John have?

Give your answer in its simplest form

(2)

Converting between fractions and decimals

To convert a fraction to a decimal, you can simply divide the numerator by the denominator, by using short division (or a calculator).

Alternatively you can type the fraction into your calculator and change it to a decimal using the S↔D button.

Example method 1

a) Convert $\frac{2}{5}$ to a decimal.

$$5\overline{)2.^20} \quad 0.4$$

Answer: 0.4

b) Convert $\frac{4}{7}$ to a decimal.

$$7\overline{)4.^40^50^10^30^20} \quad 0.57142...$$

Answer: 0.57142...

Example method 2

a) Convert $\frac{3}{5}$ to a decimal.

$$\frac{3}{5} = 0.6$$

Answer = 0.6

b) Convert $\frac{7}{40}$ to a decimal.

$$\frac{7}{40} = 0.175$$

Answer = 0.175

Practice questions:

Convert the following fractions to decimals:

a) $\frac{3}{10}$

b) $\frac{9}{20}$

c) $\frac{7}{50}$

d) $\frac{1}{8}$

e) $\frac{15}{25}$

f) $\frac{17}{50}$

g) $\frac{5}{8}$

h) $\frac{7}{28}$

i) $\frac{38}{200}$

To convert a decimal to a fraction, you first need to convert it to a percentage by multiplying it by 100.
You then convert it to a fraction by putting it over 100, ensuring there are no decimals and that it's simplified.

Examples

a) Convert 0.57 to a fraction.

Step 1: 0.57 x 100 = 57%

Step 2: $\frac{57}{100}$

b) Convert 0.455 to a fraction.

Step 1: 0.455 x 100 = 45.5%

Step 2: $\frac{45.5}{100} = \frac{455}{1000} = \frac{91}{200}$

Practice questions:

Convert the following decimals to fractions. Give your answers in their simplest forms.

j) 0.25

k) 0.54

l) 0.22

m) 0.85

n) 0.72

o) 0.38

p) 0.125

q) 1.32

Exam question:

Convert 0.124 to a fraction.

Give your answer in its simplest form.

(2)

Converting between fractions and percentages

To convert a fraction to a percentage, you can use the S↔D button to change it to a decimal, then multiply by 100.

Alternatively you can find an equivalent fraction with a denominator of 100, since percent means out of 100, the numerator will be the percentage.

Example method 1

a) Convert $\frac{3}{5}$ to a percentage. $0.6 \times 100 = 60$

$\frac{3}{5} = 0.6$ $0.6 \times 100 = 60 \rightarrow$ **60%**

b) Convert $\frac{3}{7}$ to a percentage.

$\frac{3}{7} = 0.42857...$

$0.42857 \times 100 = 42.857 \rightarrow$ **42.86%**

Example method 2

a) Convert $\frac{3}{5}$ to a percentage.

$\frac{3}{5} = \frac{60}{100} \rightarrow$ **60%**

b) Convert $\frac{12}{40}$ to a percentage.

$\frac{12}{40} = \frac{3}{10} = \frac{30}{100} \rightarrow$ **30%**

Practice questions:

Convert the following fractions to percentages:

a) $\frac{7}{10}$

b) $\frac{7}{20}$

c) $\frac{17}{50}$

d) $\frac{3}{8}$

e) $\frac{12}{25}$

f) $\frac{18}{40}$

g) $\frac{7}{9}$

h) $\frac{5}{12}$

i) $\frac{15}{200}$

Since percentage means out of 100, to convert a percentage to a fraction, you first need to place the percentage over 100, and then simplify the fractions ensuring no decimals are in your answer.

Examples

a) Convert 38% to a fraction.

Step 1: $\frac{38}{100}$

Step 2: (Simplify) $\frac{38}{100} = \frac{19}{50}$

b) Convert 48.2 to a fraction.

Step 1: $\frac{48.2}{100}$

Step 2: (Simplify) $\frac{482}{1000} = \frac{241}{500}$

Practice questions:

Convert the following percentages to fractions. Give your answers in their simplest forms.

j) 35%

k) 40%

l) 59%

m) 85%

n) 74%

o) 37.5%

p) 42.5%

q) 8.7%

 Exam question:

Convert 6.25% to a fraction.

Give your answer in its simplest form.

(2)

Converting between decimals and percentages

To convert a percentage to a decimal, you need to <u>divide by 100</u> and remove the % symbol.

Examples
a) Convert 46% to a decimal.
$46 \div 100 = \textbf{0.46}$

b) Convert 52.7% to a decimal.
$52.7 \div 100 = \textbf{0.527}$

Practice questions:
Convert the following percentages to decimals:

a) 50%

b) 30%

c) 42%

d) 12%

e) 6%

f) 96%

g) 1.2%

h) 108%

i) 0.54%

To convert a decimal to a percentage, you need to <u>multiply by 100</u> and add the % symbol.

Examples
a) Convert 0.54 to a percentage.
$0.54 \times 100 = \textbf{54\%}$

b) Convert 0.784 to a percentage.
$0.784 \times 100 = \textbf{78.4\%}$

Practice questions:
Convert the following decimals to percentages:

j) 0.24

k) 0.62

l) 0.2

m) 0.03

n) 0.74

o) 0.9

p) 1.24

q) 0.046

r) 0.0078

If you need to compare decimals against percentages, you would need to convert them so that they are all in the same format, so either convert them all to decimals, or convert them all to percentages.

Example
Write the following in descending order: 0.24 , 28% , 0.3 , 26.5% , 0.254
Converting all to percentages: 0.24 = 24%, 0.3 = 30% , 0.254 = 25.4%
In descending order 30%, 28%, 26.5%, 25.4%, 24%

Answer = 0.3 , 28%, 26.5%, 0.254, 0.24

Practice questions:
Write the following in descending order:

s) 0.5 , 48% , 0.54 , 49.5% , 0.49

t) 0.98 , 10% , 78% , 42.5% , 1.05

u) 0.5% , 1.02 , 20% , 120% , 15.4

Exam question:
a) Write the following in ascending order: 24.8% , 0.26, 18%, 0.32, 0.175

b) Work out the difference as a decimal between the biggest and smallest values.

(2)

Ordering fractions, percentages and decimals

To order a mixture of fractions, decimals or percentages, you first need to be able to convert them, so that they are all percentages, all fractions or all decimals – which ever is easiest to do.

Converting everything to fractions is often the most effective, as both decimals and percentages have denominators as powers of 10, whereas fractions like $\frac{2}{7}$ are difficult to convert to decimals/percentages.

Example

Order the following in ascending order: 0.72 $\frac{3}{4}$ 74%

Firstly convert decimals and percentage to fractions, so 0.72 becomes $\frac{72}{100}$ and 74% becomes $\frac{74}{100}$.

Now try to find an equivalent fraction for $\frac{3}{4}$ with a denominator of 100, so $\frac{3}{4} = \frac{3(\times25)}{4(\times25)} = \frac{75}{100}$

In order gives $\frac{72}{100}, \frac{74}{100}, \frac{75}{100}$, but since the question asked you to write 0.72 , $\frac{3}{4}$ and 74% in order:

Your answer will be → 0.72 , 74% , $\frac{3}{4}$

Practice questions:

Order the following in ascending order:

a) $\frac{9}{25}, 30\%, \frac{7}{20}, 0.38$

b) $\frac{4}{25}, 0.13, \frac{3}{20}, 17\%$

c) $10\%, 0.09, \frac{3}{25}, \frac{1}{20}$

d) $0.24, \frac{6}{20}, 25\%, \frac{62}{200}$

Example – Using decimals

Order the following in ascending order: $\frac{29}{40}$ 0.72 74%

Since the denominator of the fraction doesn't go nicely into 100, it is easier to change to decimals.

So $\frac{29}{40} = 0.725$ $74\% = 74 \div 100 = 0.74$ Use zeros as place holders to compare: 0.725, 0.720, 0.740

In order gives 0.720, 0.725, 0.740, but since the question asked you to write $\frac{29}{40}$, 0.72 and 74% in order:

Your answer will be → 0.72 , $\frac{29}{40}$, 74%

Practice questions:

Order the following in ascending order:

e) $\frac{9}{25}, 0.3, \frac{15}{40}, 37\%$

f) $\frac{81}{100}, 0.827, \frac{103}{125}, 83\%$

g) $\frac{17}{50}, 0.3, \frac{11}{30}, 0.37$

h) $\frac{7}{20}, 34\%, \frac{23}{60}, 0.38$

Exam question: Write the following numbers in ascending order: $\boxed{\frac{11}{25}}$ $\boxed{42\%}$ $\boxed{0.38}$ $\boxed{\frac{24}{60}}$ $\boxed{\frac{1}{3}}$

....   (2)

Introduction to percentages

A percentage is an amount out of 100.
100% is the full amount, so if you want to calculate 50%, then you just need to halve the given amount. **50%**

Examples

a) Calculate 50% of 40.
$40 \div 2 = \textbf{20}$

b) Calculate 50% of 36.
$36 \div 2 = \textbf{20}$

c) Calculate 50% of 9.
$9 \div 2 = \textbf{4.5}$

d) Calculate 50% of 43.
$43 \div 2 = \textbf{21.5}$

Practice questions (Set A):
Calculate

a) 50% of 8

b) 50% of 22

c) 50% of 48

d) 50% of 30

e) 50% of 35

f) 50% of 47

g) 50% of 57

h) 50% of 123

i) 50% of 229

Since 100% is the full amount, if you want to calculate 25%, then you just need to halve the given amount to get 50%, and then halve it again to get 25%. Alternatively – you can divide by 4. **25%**

Examples

a) Calculate 25% of 40
$40 \div 2 = 20, \ 20 \div 2 = \textbf{10}$

b) Calculate 25% of 36
$36 \div 4 = \textbf{9}$

c) Calculate 25% of 18
$18 \div 4 = \textbf{4.5}$

d) Calculate 25% of 46
$46 \div 4 = \textbf{11.5}$

Practice questions (Set B):
Calculate:

a) 25% of 60

b) 25% of 92

c) 25% of 124

d) 25% of 72

e) 25% of 148

f) 25% of 10

g) 25% of 66

h) 25% of 126

i) 25% of 700

If you want to calculate 10%, then you just need to divide the given amount by 10. **10%**

Examples

a) Calculate 10% of 40
$40 \div 10 = \textbf{4}$

b) Calculate 10% of 36
$36 \div 10 = \textbf{3.6}$

c) Calculate 10% of 92
$92 \div 10 = \textbf{9.2}$

d) Calculate 10% of 210
$210 \div 10 = \textbf{21}$

Practice questions (Set C):
Calculate:

a) 10% of 20

b) 10% of 80

c) 10% of 75

d) 10% of 320

e) 10% of 46

f) 10% of 5.4

g) 10% of 3

h) 10% of 42.7

i) 10% of 30.4

Exam question:
10% of the students in a school have blond hair.
There are 1420 students in the school in total.
How many students have blond hair?

(1)

24

Harder percentages without a calculator

1% is one hundredth of 100% (the full amount). So to calculate 1%, we need to divide the amount by 100.

Examples
a) Find 1% of 1300.

1300 ÷ 100 = 13, So 1% of 1300 = **13**

b) Example: Find 1% of £135.

135 ÷ 100 = 1.35, so 1% of £135 = **£1.35**

Practice questions:
Calculate 1% of:

a) 800

b) 6000

c) 2400

d) 18000

e) 200

f) 420

g) 33000

h) 905

i) 780

j) 2

k) 49

l) 5.8

We can use the percentages we know to build up to more challenging percentages.
For example: If we can work out 50%, 10% and 1% of a value, then by adding these – we can make 61%

Examples
a) Find 61% of 800

61% = 50% + 10% + 1% → 50% = 400 , 10% = 80, 1% = 8
So 61% = 400 + 80 + 8 = **488**

b) Find 30% of 90

30% = 10% + 10% + 10% → 10% = 9
So 30% = 9 + 9 + 9 = **27**

Practice questions:
Calculate:

m) 60% of 80

n) 11% of 40

o) 20% of 130

p) 51% of 70

q) 30% of 160

r) 40% of 95

s) 15% of 580

t) 26% of 220

If you can calculate 1%, then any percentage can be calculated. e.g 26% = 1% multiplied by 26.

Examples
a) Find 63% of 800,   1% = 8, so 63% = 8 x 63 = **504**   b) Find 37% of 600,   1% = 6, so 37% = 6 x 37 = **222**

Practice questions:
Calculate:

u) 14% of 300

v) 32% of 900

w) 24% of 150

x) 37% of 200

y) 68% of 700

z) 8% of 76

Exam question:
There are 800 students at Springbank School.
44% of the students at the school are girls.
How many boys are at the school?

(3)

Increasing and decreasing by a percentage

To increase a number by a percentage, you can calculate the percentage of the amount, and then add it onto the original amount.

Example

Increase £80 by 20%

Step 1: Work out 20% of £80   (80 ÷ 100 x 20)   = £16
Step 2: Add this amount to the original (80 + 16)   = **£96**

Practice questions:

Increase the amounts shown by the given percentages.

a) £40 by 10%

b) £42 by 50%

c) £80 by 25%

d) £30 by 20%

e) £40 by 75%

f) £54 by 10%

g) £30 by 25%

h) £70 by 5%

i) £58 by 30%

j) £54 by 3%

k) £45 by 15%

l) £24 by 0.5%

To decrease a number by a percentage, you can calculate the percentage of the amount, and then subtract it off the original amount.

Example

Decrease £80 by 15%

Step 1: Work out 15% of £80   (80 ÷ 100 x 15)   = £12
Step 2: Add this amount to the original (80 – 12)   = **£68**

Practice questions:

Decrease the amounts shown by the given percentages.

m) £60 by 50%

n) £70 by 10%

o) £76 by 50%

p) £120 by 25%

q) £72 by 25%

r) £70 by 5%

s) £50 by 75%

t) £84 by 10%

u) £35 by 50%

v) £30 by 5%

w) £84 by 3%

x) £168 by 15%

Exam question:

An office buys 400 reems of paper. Each reem of paper costs £2.40.
A 14% discount is applied to any invoice if the spending is over £750.

Work out the total invoice amount for the paper.

(2)

One number as a percentage of another

To express one number as a percentage of another, we need to divide the first number by the second number, and then multiply by 100. This is the same method as changing a fraction to a percentage.

Examples

a) What is 24 out of 40 as a percentage?

Step 1: $24 \div 40 = 0.60$
Step 2: $0.60 \times 100 = \textbf{60\%}$

or using fractions $\frac{24}{40} = 0.6 = \textbf{60\%}$

b) A 250g cake contains 90g of sugar.
What percentage of the cake is sugar?

Step 1: $90 \div 250 = 0.36$
Step 2: $0.36 \times 100 = \textbf{36\%}$

or using fractions $\frac{90}{250} = 0.36 = \textbf{36\%}$

Practice questions:

Write the following as a percentage:

a) 43 out of 100

b) 53 out of 100

c) 11 out of 50

d) 42 out of 50

e) 6 out of 10

f) 13 out of 20

g) 16 out of 40

h) 24 out of 80

i) 9 out of 12

j) 10 out of 42

k) 2.5 out of 20

l) 3.2 out of 5

Sometimes when asked to find one number as a percentage of another, the first figure is larger. If this is the case, the process is the same, but your answer will be greater than 100%.

Examples

a) What is 60 out of 40 as a percentage?

Step 1: $60 \div 40 = 1.5$
Step 2: $1.5 \times 100 = \textbf{150\%}$

or using fractions
$\frac{60}{40} = 1.5 = \textbf{150\%}$

Practice questions:

Write the following as a percentage:

m) 300 out of 100

n) 80 out of 40

o) 20 out of 15

p) 22 out of 10

q) 55 out of 44

r) 140 out of 80

Exam question:
Write 18 as a percentage of 22.
Give your answer to 1 decimal place.

(2)

Rounding to integers, tens, hundreds and thousands

When rounding numbers, we need to look at the first digit after the place value we are rounding to.
If it is 5 or more, we must round the final place value up by 1, and remove any other digits afterwards.
If it is less than 5, we leave the place value as it is, and remove the digits afterwards.
Remember that zero place holders may be required when removing digits after rounding.

Example – rounding to whole numbers

a) 43.2 to the nearest whole number.   **Answer = 43**

The number after the units column (3) is 2. Since it is **less than 5**, you leave the unit value as a 3 and remove the 2 after the decimal point.

b) 23.62 to the nearest whole number.   **Answer = 24**

The number after the units column (3) is 6. Since it is **5 or greater**, you raise the value to 4 and remove the numbers after the decimal point.

Practice questions (Set A):
Round the following values to the nearest whole number:

a) 2.4

b) 3.8

c) 14.7

d) 42.28

e) 55.91

f) 18.75

g) 91.09

h) 219.92

i) 199.12

j) 102.58

k) 99.509

l) 0.199

Example – rounding to nearest ten, hundred or thousand

a) 647 to the nearest ten.   **Answer = 650**

The number after the tens (7) is **5 or greater**, so you raise the value of 4 (tens unit) to 5, remove the 7 and replace it with a zero place holder.

b) 8412 to the nearest 100   **Answer = 8400**

The number after the hundreds (1) is **less than 5**, so keep the value of 4. Remove the digits after the 4, and replace with them with zero place holders.

Practice questions (Set B):
Round the following values to the nearest **ten**:

a) 45

b) 63

c) 29

d) 149

e) 253

f) 1,358

Round the following values to the nearest **hundred**:

g) 532

h) 866

i) 630

j) 4,729

k) 68,529

l) 99,851

Round the following values to the nearest **thousand**:

m) 6,329

n) 8,609

o) 13,247

p) 10,913

q) 373,052

r) 800,942

Exam question:
A concert venue has a capacity of 2500 seats. Each seat ticket costs £38.75.
Work out the total income from ticket sales if the venue is full.
Give your answer to the nearest £1000.

(3)

Rounding numbers to decimal places

To round to decimal places you round as before but you keep some digits after the decimal point.
Rounding to two decimal places means you need to keep two digits after the decimal place.
Remember that zero place holders may be required when removing digits after rounding.

HINT: When rounding to decimal places, ensure that your answer has exactly the number of decimal places the question has asked for, even if it is a zero.

Examples – rounding to decimal places

a) 4.52 to 1 decimal place   **Answer = 4.5**

The number after the 1st decimal place column (5) is 2. Since it is **less than 5**, you leave the 1st decimal place value as a 5 and remove the 2 after it.

b) 2.763 to 1 decimal place   **Answer = 2.8**

The number after the 1st decimal place column (7) is 6. Since it is **5 or greater**, you raise the 1st decimal place value (7) to 8 and remove the digits after it.

c) 2.704 to 2 decimal places   **Answer = 2.70**

The number after the 2nd decimal place column (0) is 4. Since it is **less than 5**, you leave the 2nd decimal place value as a 0, but it must be left to show that you have rounded it to 2 decimal places.

d) 4.298 to 2 decimal places   **Answer = 4.30**

The number after the 2nd decimal place column (9) is 8. Since it is **5 or more**, you raise the 2nd decimal place value to a 0 and therefore increase 1st decimal place from a 2 to a 3.

Practice questions:

Round the following values to **1 decimal place**:

a) 4.58	b) 7.519	c) 42.583	d) 74.682
e) 5.032	f) 86.49	g) 40.806	h) 547.86
i) 0.798	j) 1.99	k) 24.97	l) 4.012

Round the following values to **2 decimal places**:

a) 2.578	b) 0.781	c) 7.8512	d) 12.7072
e) 8.092	f) 2.504	g) 24.348	h) 33.0653
i) 2.089	j) 0.4981	k) 1.1984	l) 3.9956

Round the following values to 3 **decimal places**:

a) 5.36542	b) 4.62021	c) 4.35053
d) 45.68351	e) 0.05728	f) 16.73561
g) 54.0296	h) 6.29967	i) 13.9996

Exam question:

Pi is given as 3.14159265358979323846.....

Round pi to   a) 2 decimal places.

b) 4 decimal places.   (2)

Time

To change from 12 hour to 24 hour clock you need to add 12 hours if the time is pm. If the time is am you need to make sure the 24 hour clock has a zero in front of a 1 digit number.

Example

a) Change 5.47am to 24 hour clock. **05:47**

b) Change 5.47pm to 24 clock. **17:47**
(5 + 12 = 17)

c) Change 11:20 to 12 hour clock. **11.20am**

d) Change 19.50 to 12 hour clock. **7:50pm**
(19 - 12 = 7)

Don't forget am/pm

Practice questions:

Change to 24 hour clock:

a) 8.40am

b) 8.40pm

c) 10.30am

d) 7.16pm

e) 11.53pm

f) 12.24am

Change to 24 hour clock:

g) 22:16

h) 05:35

i) 12:35

j) 13:22

k) 16:54

l) 00:21

m) 11:03

n) 18:47

When working with time you have to be careful with hours and minutes. It is easier to attempt the questions manually than with a calculator.

Example

A film starts at 5.50pm and lasts 2 hours and 35 minutes. What time does the film finish?

+10mins +25mins +2hours

5.50pm 6pm 6.25pm 8.25pm **Answer: 8.25pm**

Deal with the minutes first. You need to add 10 minutes to get to the next full hour then an extra 25 minutes to make up 35 minutes in total.

Practice questions:

Work out the time each film finishes:

o) Start: 8.40am
Duration: 2 hours 30 mins

p) Start: 15:35
Duration: 3 hours 40 mins

q) Start: 6.42pm
Duration: 4 hours 55 mins

r) Start: 11.27am
Duration: 2 hours 48 mins

s) Start: 14:39
Duration: 4 hours 27 mins

t) Start: 22:17
Duration: 3 hours 54 mins

u) Start: 11.42pm
Duration: 4 hours 26 mins

Exam question:

Marvin watches a film.
The film lasted 3 hours 28 minutes. It finished at 18:09.
What time did the film start?

(2)

Time tables

Timetables allow you to plan a journey.
Each column represents a different bus or train.
You read down the column to see the time it arrives at each stop. The times given are given in 24 hour format.

Pudsey	0752	1135	1530	1958
Gamecock Inn	0803	1147	1542	2007
Copley Hill	0814	1156	1554	2015
Corn Exchange	0827	1210	1609	2027
Coldcotes	0843	1225	1626	2039
Seacroft	0852	1234	1636	2048

Example: I arrived at Coldcotes at 16:26.
What time did I leave Pudsey?
Find the time on the table and go up to locate Pudsey
15:30

Practice questions:
Using the table provided:

Gospel Lane	0655	0915	1116	1334	1642	-
Green Village	0707	0927	1127	1346	1654	2112
College Arms	0716	0936	1137	1355	-	2119
Mosely Village	0728	0945	1145	1404	1713	-
Priory Road	0738	0952	1152	1411	1722	2129
Five Ways	0748	0959	1200	1418	1730	2140
Broad Street	0756	1001	1202	1420	-	2142

a) What time does the first bus leave Green Village?

b) What time does the 2nd bus leave Gospel Lane?

c) What time does the last bus leave College Arms?

d) What time does the 0915 from Gospel Lane arrive at Five Ways?

e) What time does the 1145 from Mosely Village arrive at Broad Street?

f) How many buses arrive at Broad Street after 12pm?

g) What is latest bus you can catch from Gospel Lane to get to Priory Road before 1200?

h) How long does it take the 0707 bus from Green Village to get to Broad Street?

i) If you arrive at Green Village bus stop at 4pm, how long do you need to wait for the next bus to Broad Street?

Exam question:
a) Where did you catch a bus from if your journey time was 9 minutes and you got off at Broad Street at 1001?

b) John catches the 6:55am bus from Gospel lane to Mosely Village. He spend 3 hours at Mosely Village and then catches the next bus to Broad Street, what time did he get to Broad Street?

(2)

When working with money, you need to make sure your calculations are all done in the same denomination, i.e in pounds or pence. Convert values at the beginning of your calculations to avoid complications later.

Example (Totals)

Jim buys: 2 cans of coke for 70p each,
1 sandwich for £2.30 and 1 muffin for £1.15.
Work out the total cost.

Step 1: Change all the amounts to pounds → Can of coke = £0.70
Step 2: Use column method to add them up.

```
  0.70
  0.70
  2.30
+1.15
  4.85
```

Answer = £4.85

Practice questions:

Calculate the total if the following items were bought from CoCo's Café:

a) 2 x Chips, 1 Burger and 1 Toast.

b) 2 x Chips, 1 Lasagne and 3 x Toast.

c) 3 x Burgers, 4 x Chips and 1 Hot dog.

d) 5 x Chips, 5 x Burgers and 3 x Hot dogs.

Menu

Chips	80p
Lasagne	£2.60
Burger	£2.00
Hot Dog	£1.40
Toast	50p

Example (Change)

Jim buys: 2 cans of coke for 60p each,
1 Burger for £2.90 and a portion of chips for £1.65.
Work out the total change when Jim paid with a £10 note.

Step 1: Change all the amounts to pounds → Can of coke = £0.60
Step 2: Use column method to add them up.
Step 3: Subtract the total from £10.00   10.00 – 5.75 = 4.25

```
  0.60
  0.60
  2.90
+1.65
  5.75
```

Answer = £4.25

Practice questions:

Calculate the change from £20 if the following items were bought from the Diner:

e) 1 x Chips, 2 Salads and 3 x Toast.

f) 2 x Chips, 3 Lattes and 2 x Toast.

g) 3 x Paninis, 3 x Chips and 4 x Lattes.

h) 4 x Chips, 4 x Salads, 2 x Paninis and 1 Toast.

Menu

Chips	75p
Salad	£1.45
Latte	£2.20
Panini	£1.90
Toast	55p

Exam question:

Marley has a job which pays £16 an hour after all deductions.
She wants to buy a new television costing £750.
If she receives £16 per hour, how many hours does she need to work,
to earn enough to buy the ticket?

(2)

Terms, expressions, equations, formulas and identities

A **term** is a single mathematical expression. It may be a single number or variable (letter), or several variables multiplied. It can also be a number multiplied by a variable. The number in front of a variable is called a coefficient.

An **expression** is a set of terms combined using the operations $+, -,$ x or $\div$, for example. $4x - 3$ or $x^2 - 2$ It must involve a minimum of two terms/numbers/ variables or combination of that has an operation between them. **It does NOT have an equal sign.**

Examples:

Which of the following are terms of the expression $4x^2 + 7x + 32$?

a) $4x^2$ **Answer: Yes**   c) x^2 **Answer: No**   e) $4x^2 + 7x$ **Answer: No**

b) $7x$ **Answer: Yes**   d) 32 **Answer: Yes**   f) $7x + 32$ **Answer: No**

An **equation** is a mathematical expression that contains an **equals** symbol. An equation only has one variable and an equals sign, so therefore *can* be solved to find the value of the variable (letter).

A **formula** is a fact or a rule which usually connects two or more variables and numbers with an equal sign. A formula *cannot* be solved without being given some values to substitute into it.

Examples:

Is it an expression, equation or formula?

a) $A = lw$ **Answer: Formula**   c) $x^2 = 16$ **Answer: Equation**   e) πr^2 **Answer: Expression**

b) $x + 2 = 6$ **Answer: Equation**   d) $3x - 5$ **Answer: Expression**   f) $s = ut$ **Answer: Formula**

An **identity** is like an equation which is always true, no matter what values are substituted. e.g. 2x + 3x = 5x
An identity can sometimes be easily identified as the = sign is replaced with the ≡ sign. e.g. 2x + 3x ≡ 5x

Practice questions:

Classify each of the following as either an expression, equation, formula or identity.

a) $A = wl$

b) $2x = 4$

c) $5x^2$

d) $c = \pi d$

e) $6a = 4a + 2a$

f) $2a + 5c$

g) $6ab$

h) $6c + d = e$

i) $4a + 2 = a$

j) $4a = 2b$

k) $6x^2 = 2x$

l) $2(a + b) \equiv 2a + 2b$

m) $5a = 2a + 3$

n) $x = 2wl$

Exam question:

One of the following is an expression, one is an equation and one is a formula.

State which is which:

       A) $x^2 + 3x - 28$ B) $P = 2(a + b)$ C) $20 + 5x = 20$

(2)

Simplifying expressions (adding/subtracting)

Expressions often have more than one term, but sometimes those terms can be simplified.
If the terms have the same letter or collection of letters, then they can be added or subtracted.

Examples

Simplify these expressions:

a) $4x + 3x$ **Answer : 7x**   Terms have the same letter, so you can add the coefficients (4 + 3).

b) $6x - 2x$ **Answer : 4x**   Terms have the same letter, so you can subtract the coefficients (6 - 2).

c) $7a + 4a + a$ **Answer : 12a**   You need to know that the coefficient of a is **1**, so it will be 7 + 4 + **1**

Practice questions:

Simplify the following expressions:

a) $5x + 2x$

b) $6y - 3y$

c) $4x - x$

d) $3x + x + x$

e) $6c + 2c - c$

f) $8a + 2a + 3a$

g) $45a - 8a - a$

h) $2x + 5x - 7x$

Sometimes terms have different or no letters. You must look carefully at the sign in front of each term to make sure you complete the correct operations. Numbers are treated separate to anything with a letter.

Examples

Simplify these expressions:

a) $4x + 2x + 3$ **Answer : 6x + 3**

b) $6x + 2y - 2x$ **Answer : 4x + 2y**

c) $4x + 8y - 2x + 6$ **Answer : 2x + 8y + 6**

d) $12y - 2x + 5 + 8y + 12x$ **Answer : 20y + 10x + 5**

Practice questions:

Simplify the following expressions:

i) $5x + 2y + 2y + x$

j) $6y + 5x + y + 2x$

k) $4x + 6 + 3x + 2y$

l) $8x + 3y + 2x - y$

m) $12x + 6y - x - 2y$

n) $8x - 2y + 2x + 6$

o) $13a - 2b + 2a - 2b$

p) $8s - 2t + 6 + 4t$

q) $16 + 2y - 2x + x - 9$

r) $5x + 4 - 2y - x - 13$

Exam question:

The diagram shows an algebraic number pyramid.
Each brick is equal to the sum of the two bricks below it.
Find the expressions for the two missing bricks.

	10a + 7b	
5a + 3b		
2a + b	3a + 2b	

(2)

34

Simplifying expressions (multiplying/dividing)

When multiplying expressions you multiply the numbers together. If you are multiplying with the same letter, you need to use powers in your solution. All letters should be dealt with separately.

Examples

Simplify these expressions:

a) 3a x 5b   **Answer : 15ab**   Terms have different letters, so you can only multiply the coefficients (3 x 5)

b) 6c x 2c   **Answer : 12c²**   Terms have the same letter, so you can use powers (c x c = c²)

c) 8wy² x 3wy **Answer : 24w²y³**   You need to treat each letter and number separately (8 x 3, w x w, y² x y)

Practice questions:

Simplify the following expressions:

a) $5x \times 2y$

b) $6a \times 2b$

c) $4x \times 2w$

d) $5u \times 3v$

e) $6t \times t$

f) $8a \times a$

g) $3a \times 3a$

h) $2x \times 5xy$

i) $3d \times 2c \times 4d$

j) $a \times 2a \times 3a$

k) $4a \times 2b^2 \times 2a$

l) $8a^2b \times 2ab^2$

When dividing expressions you divide the numbers. If you are dividing the same letter, you need to subtract powers (using index laws). All letters should be dealt with separately.

Examples

Simplify these expressions:

a) $\dfrac{10ab}{2}$ **Answer : 5ab**   Only the number can be divided (10 ÷ 2 = 5). No other letters to consider.

b) $\dfrac{15a^2b}{5ab}$ **Answer : 3a**   Here we divide (15 ÷ 5 = 3). Then $a^2 \div a = a$, followed by b ÷ b = 1
Since anything multiplied by 1 is the same, the b's effectively "cancel out".

Practice questions:

Simplify the following expressions:

m) $\dfrac{30a}{10}$

n) $\dfrac{80z}{4}$

o) $\dfrac{24x^2}{6}$

p) $\dfrac{40a^2}{2a^2}$

q) $\dfrac{50a^2}{10a}$

r) $\dfrac{12ab^2}{3ab}$

s) $\dfrac{30t^2}{5t}$

t) $\dfrac{15c}{30c}$

u) $\dfrac{12}{24a}$

v) $\dfrac{15b}{45a}$

w) $\dfrac{36a}{48a^2}$

x) $\dfrac{25x}{35x^2}$

Exam question:

The diagram below shows an algebraic number pyramid.
Each brick is equal to the product of the two bricks below it.
Find expressions for the two missing bricks.

(2)

35

Expanding single brackets

To expand a bracket you must **multiply** everything inside the bracket by the term on the outside of the bracket. You should be left with the same number of terms that exists within the bracket.

Examples:

a) Expand: $4(x + 3)$

    Multiply the x by 4: $4x$

    Multiply the +3 by 4: $+12$ **Answer : $4x + 12$**

b) Expand: $2x(x - 5)$

    Multiply the x by $2x$: $2x^2$

    Multiply -5 by $2x$: $-10x$ **Answer : $4x + 12$**

c) Expand: $-7(2x - 3)$

    Multiply the $2x$ by -7: $-14x$

    Multiply -7 by $2x$:   21   **Answer : $-14x + 21$**

Please note: It is important that you check the signs of the terms both inside and outside of the bracket.

Practice questions:

Expand the following expressions:

a) $5(x + 2)$

b) $3(a - 4)$

c) $2(10 - y)$

d) $8(4 - 3y)$

e) $7(3x + 8)$

f) $5(4a - 7)$

g) $9(11 - 3y)$

h) $y(y - 3)$

i) $x(x + 2)$

j) $6a(a - 9)$

k) $2y(6y + 7)$

l) $x(8 - x)$

m) $4x(12 - 5x)$

n) $6(2x + 5y)$

o) $2a(a + 8)$

p) $a(b - 2a)$

q) $a(a^2 - 2a)$

r) $-4(x + 5)$

s) $-9(x - 8)$

t) $-x(3x - 5)$

u) $-y(7 - 5y)$

v) $x^2(6x + 4)$

w) $2ab(a + 13)$

x) $a^2b(3b + 6a)$

y) $7xy(y^2 - 7x)$

z) $-x^3(5y - 8x)$

Exam question:

Expand: $8x^2y(5x - 4y)$

(2)

To solve an equation you need to get the unknown (letter) on its own. To do this we need to work backwards using inverses to re-arrange it.

Examples – adding/subtracting

Adding and subtracting are inverses of each other.

a) Solve: $x + 7 = 9$ To get x on its own – you need to subtract 7 from "both" sides.

$x = 9 - 7$ x is now on its own, so this is our solution.

$x = 2$

Answer : $x = 2$

b) Solve: $x - 5 = 3$ To get x on its own – you need to add 5 to "both" sides.

$x = 3 + 5$ x is now on its own, so this is our solution.

$x = 8$

Answer : $x = 8$

Practice questions:

Solve the following equations:

a) $x + 7 = 12$

d) $4 + a = 10$

g) $6 + x = -2$

b) $x - 5 = 10$

e) $6 + a = 42$

h) $c - 7 = -5$

c) $x + 9 = 21$

f) $8 = x - 2$

i) $7 + a = -2$

Examples – multiplying/dividing

Multiplying and dividing are inverses of each other.

a) Solve: $5x = 20$ To get x on its own – you need to divide by 5 on "both" sides.

$x = 20 \div 5$ x is now on its own, so this is our solution.

$x = 4$

Answer : $x = 4$

b) Solve: $\frac{x}{4} = 3$ To get x on its own – you need to multiply "both" sides by 4.

$x = 3 \times 4$ x is now on its own, so this is our solution.

$x = 12$

Answer : $x = 12$

Practice questions:

Solve the following equations:

j) $4x = 40$

m) $\frac{x}{5} = 2$

p) $-4x = 24$

k) $7x = 35$

n) $\frac{x}{6} = 3$

q) $\frac{x}{-4} = 3$

l) $2x = 20$

o) $\frac{x}{4} = -2$

r) $-3x = -18$

Exam question:

The shape shown is a square.

Find the value of x in the diagram.

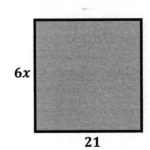

$6x$

21

(1)

Solving two step equations

To solve an equation you need to get the letter on its own. To do this you need to work backwards using inverses. You need to inverse the number that is on its own first.

Example:

Solve: $3x + 2 = 11$　　　　　**Step 1:** The 2 is on its own so we inverse this first by subtracting 2
　　　　$3x = 11 - 2$　　　　　　　　Make sure you do the same to both sides
　　　　　$3x = 9$　　　　**Step 2:** The inverse of multiplying by 3 is dividing by 3
　　　　　$x = 9 \div 3$　　　　　　　Divide both sides by 3
　　　　　$x = 3$

Practice questions:

Solve:

a) $2x + 4 = 8$

b) $2x + 3 = 13$

c) $3x + 1 = 10$

d) $4x + 2 = 18$

e) $3x - 7 = 20$

f) $5x - 4 = 31$

g) $8x + 7 = 39$

h) $7x - 5 = 37$

i) $9x - 2 = 70$

j) $3a + 15 = 48$

k) $6t - 25 = 65$

l) $6x + 7 = 1$

m) $3c - 7 = -16$

n) $-5g - 13 = -3$

The diagram is a square with its dimensions shown.
Find the value of x.

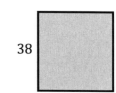

38

$11x + 5$

(2)

Solving two step equations (2)

Practice questions:

Solve:

a) $\frac{x}{5} + 1 = 5$

b) $\frac{x}{2} + 4 = 5$

c) $\frac{x}{4} + 3 = 9$

d) $\frac{f}{12} + 2 = 9$

e) $\frac{x}{2} - 9 = 9$

f) $\frac{a}{8} + 6 = 2$

g) $\frac{h}{11} - 5 = 6$

h) $\frac{t}{13} - 6 = -8$

Practice questions:

Solve:

i) $\frac{x+4}{3} = 3$

j) $\frac{x+1}{4} = 5$

k) $\frac{x-4}{2} = 4$

l) $\frac{x-2}{4} = 6$

m) $\frac{a-9}{7} = 9$

n) $\frac{x+3}{2} = 4.5$

o) $\frac{s-1}{4} = 1.25$

p) $\frac{x+2}{4} = -5$

Exam question:

Solve $4 + \frac{x}{3} = 12$

(2)

Forming expressions and equations

With a lot of maths problems, it helps if you are able to write the problem as an expression or equation with letters and numbers. Once in these forms, you can apply maths techniques to solve them.

Examples – setting up expressions

a) A number increased by 5: We can call a number: x, therefore x increased by 5 is $x + 5$

b) Write an expression for the cost of 8 apples: We can call one apple: **a**, so eight apples is: **8 x a = 8a**

c) The number of people on a bus if 2 people get off: Call the number of people on the bus: **n**
   If two people get off: **n – 2**

Practice questions:

Write the following as an expression:

a) There are n people on a bus: 5 people get on.

b) A number x is decreased by 4.

c) A number x is doubled and 5 is added to it.

d) The cost of a banana is b, the cost of 5 bananas.

e) There are n people on a bus: 20% of people get off.

f) A number x is halved.

g) A number a is increased by 5, then doubled.

h) A number c is squared before adding 2.

When setting up equations, you need to remember the equals sign so you can solve it.

Examples – setting up equations

a) A number decreased by 5 equals 9: You can call a number: x, therefore $x - 5 = 9$

b) 6 bananas cost £2: You can call one banana: **b**, so six bananas is **6b**, therefore **6b = 2**

c) The perimeter of a square equals 34cm: Call the side of the square: x. Perimeter $= x + x + x + x = 4x$
   Therefore $4x = 34$

Practice questions:

Write an equation for the following:

i) There are n people on a bus, 5 people get on.
   There are now 12 people on the bus.

j) A number n decreased by 15 is now 22.

k) A square has side length x, its perimeter is 24cm.

l) A number x is multiplied by 2, then increased
   by 7. It is now equal to 17.

m) 4 apples cost 40p less than £2.00.

n) A rectangle has side lengths $3x$ and x,
   it's perimeter is 42cm.

Exam question:

x is a positive integer.

Write an equation for the area rectangle, given that the area is
of the rectangle is 36cm^2.

Hence, calculate the value of x.

4cm

$3x$ cm

(3)

Co-ordinates

Co-ordinates give you a position on a grid. The Cartesian coordinate system is used for GCSE. This uses an x co-ordinate for the horizontal distance from the origin, and a y co-ordinate for the vertical distance from the origin. They are written using two numbers like: (2,4)

The first number (x) tells you how far to move **right**.
The second number (y) tells you how far to move **up**.   **The centre of the grid is called the origin (0,0).**

Examples (positive only)

Plot the following co-ordinates:

a) A (5, 2)   This means we must move right 5 and up 2.
b) B (2, 3)   This means we must move right 2 and up 3.
c) C (0, 4)   This means we just go up 4 from the origin.
d) D (3, 0)   This means we must move right 3 from the origin.

Note : If the co-ordinates are negative, you go in the opposite direction. So (-2,-5) would move 2 **left**, and 5 **down**.

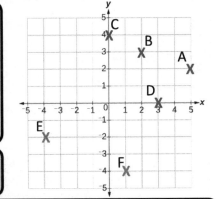

Examples (with negatives)

Plot the following co-ordinates:

e) E (−4, −2) This means we must move **left** 4 left and **down** 2.
f) F (1, -4)   This means we must move **right** 1 and **down** 4.

Practice questions:

Plot the following points on the cartesian grid and label them with the letters given.

a) A (8,5)   e) E (-4,7)

b) B (5,8)   f) F (-8,-2)

c) C (2,6)   g) G (7,-7)

d) D (7,0)   h) H (0,-5)

Write the co-ordinates of the following points from the diagram:

i) I   [   ]   m) M [   ]

j) J   [   ]   n) N [   ]

k) K   [   ]   o) O [   ]

l) L   [   ]   p) P [   ]

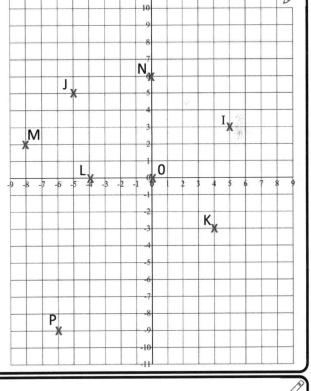

Exam question:

On the co-ordinate grid above, plot the point Q at (-3,-3)
Hence describe the type of shape formed by OJMQ

(2)

Using number sequences and describing a rule of a sequence

Sequences are a set of numbers which follow a pattern. The numbers are called terms.
The term to term rule tells you how to get to the next number.

Example :

a) What are the next three terms in the sequence?   8, 10 , 12, 14, 16... 18 20 22
                                                     +2 +2 +2 +2   +2 +2 +2

b) What are the next 3 terms in the sequence?   35, 34 , 32, 29, 25...20 14   7
                                                 −1 −2 −3 −4 −5 −6 −7

Step 1: Identify the pattern   **Step 2:** Continue the pattern for the number of values requested.

Practice questions:

Find the next three terms in the sequence:

a) 5, 7, 9, 11, 13...

b) 14, 18, 22, 26, 30...

c) 37, 32, 27, 22, 17...

d) 1, 3, 6, 10, 15...

e) 58, 53, 47, 40, 32...

f) 7, 10, 16, 25, 37...

g) 15, 12, 9, 6, 3...

h) 26, 21, 16, 11, 6...

i) 7, 14, 28, 56, 112...

j) 1, 1, 2, 3, 5, 8, 13...

Example:

a) Describe the term to term rule.   7, 12 , 17, 22, 27...   **Rule: Add 5 to the previous term.**
                                      +5 +5 +5 +5

b) Describe the term to term rule.   3, 6, 12, 24, 48...   **Rule: Multiply previous term by 2.**
                                      x2 x2 x2 x2

Step 1: Identify the pattern   **Step 2:** Write in words as simply as you can in so it cannot be 'misunderstood'.

Practice questions:

Write down the rule for each sequence:

k) 14, 17, 20, 23, 26...

l) 67, 61, 55, 49, 43...

m) 53, 64, 75, 86, 97...

n) 7, 8, 10, 13, 17...

o) 5, 10, 20, 40, 80...

p) 48, 24, 12, 6, 3...

q) 43, 36, 30, 25, 21...

r) 1, 4, 9, 16, 25...

s) -5, -12, -19, -26, -33...

t) 7, 5, 2, 3, -1, 4, -5...

Exam question:

Matches are laid out in the patterns below.
If the pattern continues, how many matches will be there be in the next two diagrams?

(2)

Inequality notation

An inequality is used to describe if one number is bigger or smaller than another.
Inequality symbols: $>$ $<$ $\leq$ $\geq$
The inequality opens up at the bigger number. If the numbers can be equal to each other a line is included under the inequality.

Example:

a) $5 > 2$ (5 is bigger than 2 so open at the 5)   b) $13 < 20$ (20 is bigger than 13 so open at the 13)

Practice questions:

True or False?

a) $6 < 4$

b) $7 < 9$

c) $9 > 7$

d) $7 < 11$

e) $7 \leq 11$

f) $8 < 8$

g) $15 \leq 5$

h) $7 \geq 7$

i) $8 \geq 9$

j) $2 < 19$

k) $23 \geq 4$

l) $13 < 9$

$x > 5$ means x is greater than 5 (6, 7, 8, 9, 10...) $x < 5$ means x is less than 5 (4, 3, 2, 1, 0...)
$x \geq 5$ means x is greater than **or equal to** 5 (**5**, 6, 7, 8, 9...)

Example:
List the first 5 integers (whole numbers) which satisfy the following inequalities:
a) $x > 9$ The inequality is opened at the x so it means x is greater than 9:   **10, 11, 12, 13, 14**
b) $x \leq 8$ The inequality is not open at the x so it means x is less than <u>or equal to</u> 8:   **8, 7, 6, 5, 4**

Practice questions:

List the first 5 integers which satisfy the following inequalities:

m) $x < 7$

n) $x \geq 4$

o) $x > 12$

p) $x \leq 15$

q) $6 < x$

r) $x \leq 2$

s) $11 \geq x$

t) $21 \leq x$

A double inequality can be used to describe if a number is between two numbers.
$3 < x \leq 7$ means x is between 3 & 7 and it can also equal 7 because the 2ⁿᵈ inequality has an equal to line.

Example:
List the integers which satisfy the following inequalities:
a) $4 < x < 8$ List all the numbers between 4 and 8:   **5, 6, 7**
b) $4 \leq x < 8$ List all the numbers between 4 and 8 but also include 4:   **4, 5, 6, 7**

Practice questions:

List the integers which satisfy the following inequalities:

u) $2 < x < 7$

v) $6 < x \leq 9$

w) $0 \leq x \leq 5$

x) $8 \leq x < 13$

y) $-2 < x \leq 4$

z) $6 < x < 8$

α) $-5 \leq x \leq 1$

β) $5 \leq x < 6$

Measuring lines with a ruler

When measuring a line with a ruler, you must make sure the end of the ruler is lined up with the end of the line, and ensure you read the correct value shown.

Examples

Measure the length of the line

Step 1: Place the ruler so 0 lines up with the end of the line.

Step 2: Read the length of the line. Remember each small line is 0.1cm.

5.9cm

Practice questions:

With a ruler, measure the length of the lines:

a)

b)

c)

d)

e)   f)   g)

Exam question:

a) Measure the length of BC

b) How much longer is BC than AB?

B _____ C

A

(2)

44

Types of angles

An angle is a measure of the space between two intersecting lines. The bigger the gap, the bigger the angle. The size of the angle also determines the name given to it. Angles are one of the five following types.

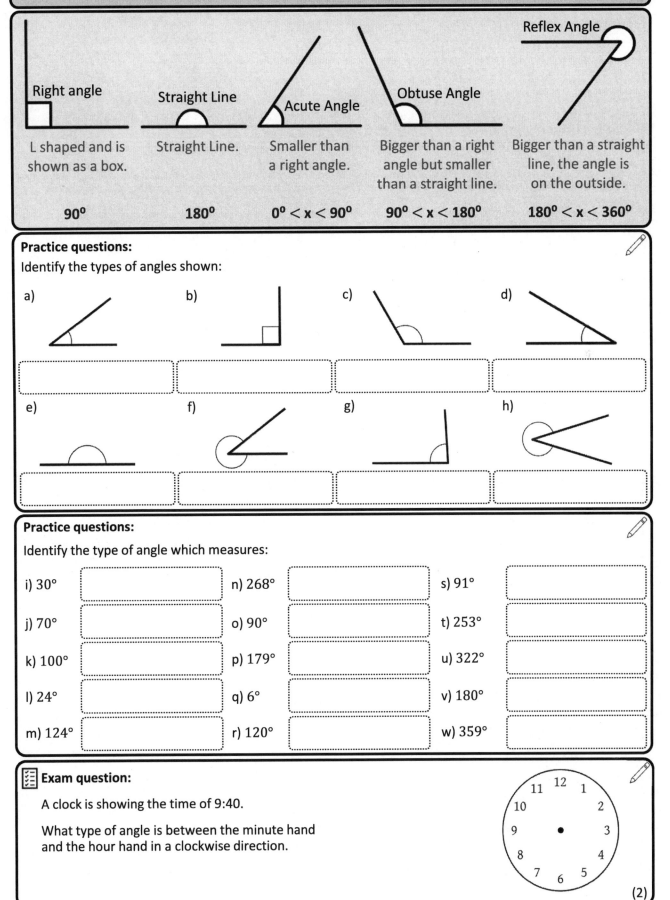

Right angle	Straight Line	Acute Angle	Obtuse Angle	Reflex Angle
L shaped and is shown as a box.	Straight Line.	Smaller than a right angle.	Bigger than a right angle but smaller than a straight line.	Bigger than a straight line, the angle is on the outside.
90°	180°	$0^\circ < x < 90^\circ$	$90^\circ < x < 180^\circ$	$180^\circ < x < 360^\circ$

Practice questions:

Identify the types of angles shown:

a)

b)

c)

d)

e)

f)

g)

h)

Practice questions:

Identify the type of angle which measures:

i) 30°

j) 70°

k) 100°

l) 24°

m) 124°

n) 268°

o) 90°

p) 179°

q) 6°

r) 120°

s) 91°

t) 253°

u) 322°

v) 180°

w) 359°

Exam question:

A clock is showing the time of 9:40.

What type of angle is between the minute hand and the hour hand in a clockwise direction.

(2)

Measuring angles with a protractor

When measuring an angle with a protractor, it's all about ensuring that you line up the cross-hairs of the protractor at the vertex of the 2 lines correctly, and ensuring you read the correct value shown.

Examples
Measure the angle between the lines given

Step 1: Place the midpoint cross-hairs (+) of the protractor on the **VERTEX** of the angle.

Step 2: Line up one line of the angle with the zero line of the protractor (where you see the number 0).

Step 3: Read the degrees where the other line crosses the number scale of the protractor (ensuring that you read the scale that "starts from zero")

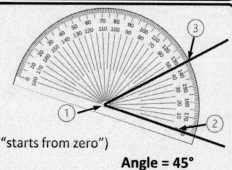

Angle = 45°

Practice questions:

With a protractor, measure the angles of labelled a to f:

a)

b)

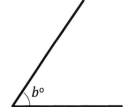

c)

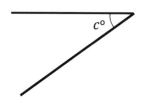

d)

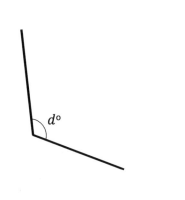

e)

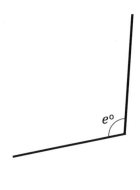

f)

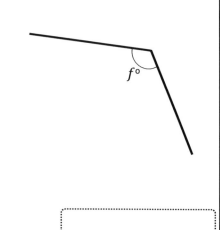

Exam question:

a) Measure the value of x

b) Hence of otherwise calculate the value of y

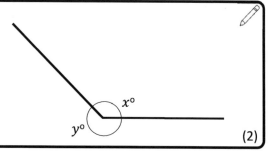

(2)

Drawing angles with a protractor

When drawing an angle with a protractor and ruler, it's all about ensuring that you line up the cross-hairs of the protractor at the end of the line, and select the correct value on the protractor.

Examples

Draw a 50° angle with a ruler and protractor

Step 1: Draw a straight line.

Step 2: Place the midpoint cross-hairs (+) of the protractor at the end of the line where you want the **VERTEX** of the angle.

Step 3: Look for 50° on the protractor and mark it with a pencil.

Step 4: Using a ruler, draw a line from the VERTEX end to the mark you had made.

Practice questions:

With a protractor and ruler, draw in the spaces provided the following angles:

a) 60°

b) 75°

c) 54°

d) 125°

e) 144°

d) 193°

e) 282°

Constructing triangles with a ruler and protractor

When constructing a triangle with a protractor and ruler, you need to start by drawing one of the sides before measuring the angle.

Example

Draw the triangle to scale with a ruler and protractor.

2.4cm
45°
3cm

Step 1: Draw the base line.
Step 2: From the base line measure the angle.
Step 3: Following the line of the angle measure the second side.
Step 4: Complete the triangle.

Step 1:

3cm

Step 2:

x

3cm

Step 3:

2.4cm
45°
3cm

Step 4:

2.4cm
45°
3cm

Practice questions:

With a protractor and ruler, construct the triangles in the spaces provided:

a)

5.9cm
30°
6cm

c)

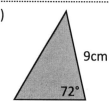
9cm
72°
7.4cm

b)

4.2cm
78°
5.5cm

Exam question:

In the space provided, construct with a ruler and protractor an accurate diagram of the following.

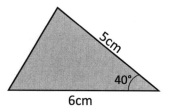
5cm
40°
6cm

(2)

When constructing a triangle with a compass and ruler, you need to start by drawing one of the sides with a ruler before using the compass.

Example

Draw the triangle to scale with a ruler and protractor.

2.4cm 2.2cm

3cm

Step 1: Draw the base line.
Step 2: Open the compass 2.4cm and draw an arc from the left of the line
Step 3: Open the compass 2.2cm and draw an arc from the right of the line
Step 4: Complete the triangle with the intersection point.

Step 1:

3cm

Step 2:

2.4cm

3cm

Step 3:

2.2cm

3cm

Step 4:

3cm

Practice questions:

With a compass and ruler, construct the triangles in the spaces provided with dimensions:

a) 6cm, 7cm and 2cm

c) 5cm, 5cm and 5cm

b) 7.5cm, 5cm and 6cm

d) 6.8cm, 5.9cm and 4.6cm

Exam question:

In the space provided, construct with a ruler and protractor an accurate diagram of the following.

3.5cm   5cm

6cm

(2)

Types of triangles

A triangle is a three sided polygon. Triangles can be classified by the size of their sides and angles.

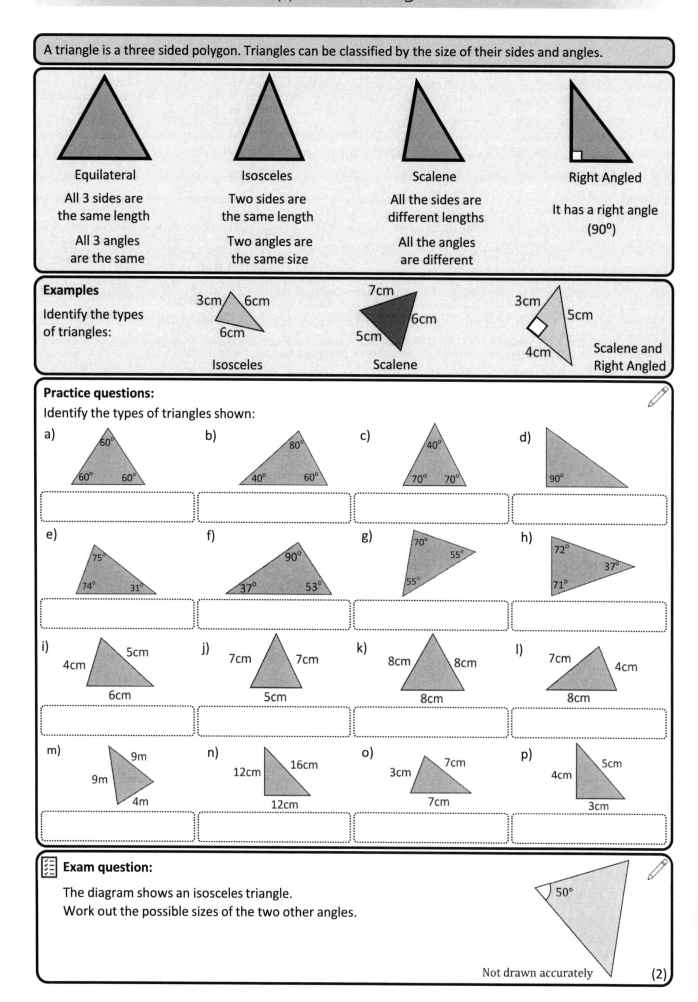

Equilateral

All 3 sides are the same length

All 3 angles are the same

Isosceles

Two sides are the same length

Two angles are the same size

Scalene

All the sides are different lengths

All the angles are different

Right Angled

It has a right angle (90º)

Examples

Identify the types of triangles:

3cm 6cm
6cm
Isosceles

7cm
6cm
5cm
Scalene

3cm 5cm
4cm
Scalene and Right Angled

Practice questions:

Identify the types of triangles shown:

a) 60° 60° 60°

b) 80° 40° 60°

c) 40° 70° 70°

d) 90°

e) 75° 74° 31°

f) 90° 37° 53°

g) 70° 55° 55°

h) 72° 37° 71°

i) 5cm 4cm 6cm

j) 7cm 7cm 5cm

k) 8cm 8cm 8cm

l) 7cm 4cm 8cm

m) 9m 9m 4m

n) 12cm 16cm 12cm

o) 3cm 7cm 7cm

p) 5cm 4cm 3cm

Exam question:

The diagram shows an isosceles triangle.
Work out the possible sizes of the two other angles.

50°

Not drawn accurately (2)

50

Types of quadrilaterals

A quadrilateral is a four sided polygon. Quadrilaterals can be classified depending their properties.

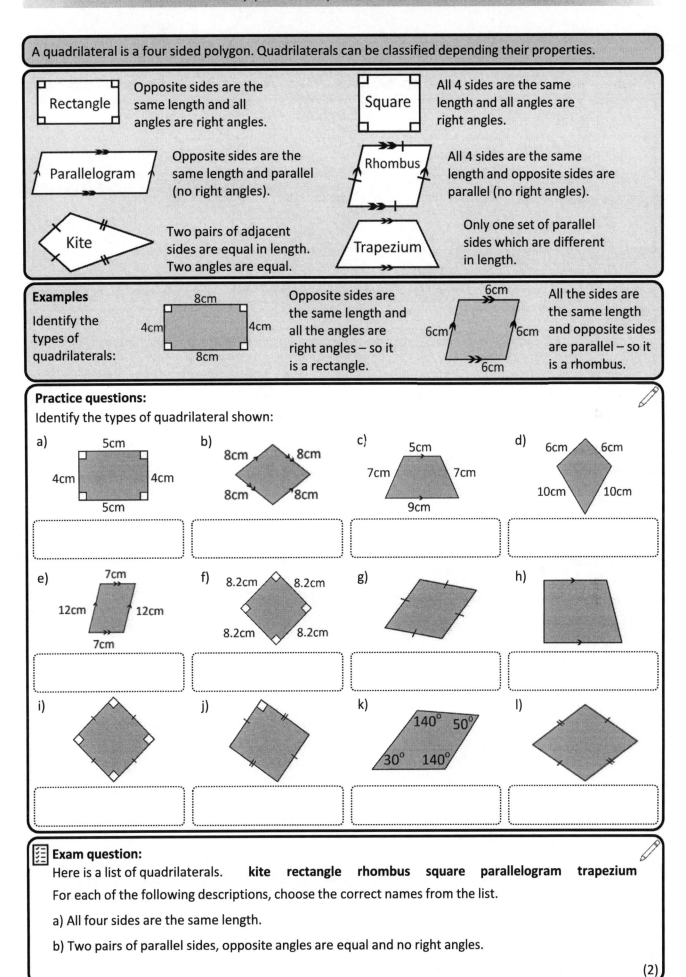

Rectangle Opposite sides are the same length and all angles are right angles.

Square All 4 sides are the same length and all angles are right angles.

Parallelogram Opposite sides are the same length and parallel (no right angles).

Rhombus All 4 sides are the same length and opposite sides are parallel (no right angles).

Kite Two pairs of adjacent sides are equal in length. Two angles are equal.

Trapezium Only one set of parallel sides which are different in length.

Examples

Identify the types of quadrilaterals:

8cm / 4cm / 4cm / 8cm — Opposite sides are the same length and all the angles are right angles – so it is a rectangle.

6cm / 6cm / 6cm / 6cm — All the sides are the same length and opposite sides are parallel – so it is a rhombus.

Practice questions:

Identify the types of quadrilateral shown:

a) 5cm / 4cm / 4cm / 5cm

b) 8cm / 8cm / 8cm / 8cm

c) 5cm / 7cm / 7cm / 9cm

d) 6cm / 6cm / 10cm / 10cm

e) 7cm / 12cm / 12cm / 7cm

f) 8.2cm / 8.2cm / 8.2cm / 8.2cm

g)

h)

i)

j)

k) 140° 50° 30° 140°

l)

Exam question:

Here is a list of quadrilaterals.   **kite   rectangle   rhombus   square   parallelogram   trapezium**

For each of the following descriptions, choose the correct names from the list.

a) All four sides are the same length.

b) Two pairs of parallel sides, opposite angles are equal and no right angles.

(2)

Missing angles in right angles and on straight lines

Angles in a right angle sum to 90°.
To find a missing angle in a right angle, subtract the known angles from 90°.

Examples

Find the missing angles (x):

Subtract the known angle from 90°

$90 - 63 = 27$

Answer: 27°

$x°$ $63°$

Subtract the known angles from 90°

$90 - 32 - 36 = 22$

Answer: 22°

$x°$ $32°$ $36°$

Practice questions:

Calculate the missing angle x:

a) $40°$ $x°$

b) $x°$ $35°$

c) $x°$ $27°$

d) $x°$ $49°$

e) $x°$ $35°$ $20°$

f) $21°$ $38°$ $x°$

g) $38.5°$ $x°$

h) $x°$ $32.1°$ $28.5°$

Angles on a straight line sum to 180°.
To find a missing angle on a straight line, subtract the known angles from 180°.

Examples

Find the missing angles (x):

Subtract the known angles from 180°
$180 - 61 - 63 = 56$

Answer: 56°

$61°$ $x°$ $63°$

Subtract the known angles from 180°
$180 - 90 - 63 = 27$

Answer: 27°

$x°$ $63°$

Practice questions:

Calculate the missing angle x:

i) $x°$ $60°$

j) $115°$ $x°$

k) $75°$ $50°$ $x°$

l) $95°$ $45°$ $x°$

m) $73°$ $x°$ $68°$

n) $x°$ $72°$ $48°$

o) $51°$ $41°$ $x°$

p) $55°$ $x°$ $49°$ $67°$

📋 **Exam question:**

Calculate the value of x.

$x°$ $33°$

(2)

Angles around a point sum to 360°.
To find a missing angle around a point, subtract the known angles from 360°.

Examples

Find the missing angles (x):

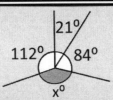

Subtract the known angles from 360°

$360 - 112 - 21 - 84 = 143$

Answer : 143°

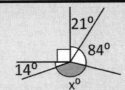

Subtract the known angles from 360°

$360 - 90 - 14 - 21 - 84$
$= 151$ **Answer : 151°**

Practice questions:

Calculate the missing angle x:

a)

b)

c)
162°   x°

d)
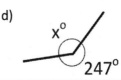

e)

f)
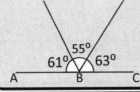

g)
130°   90°   60°   x°

h)
39°   119°   x°   129°

You may be asked to show if points form a straight line. You need to check if the angles sum to 180°.

Example

Determine if ABC is a straight line.

55°
61°   63°
A   B   C

If the angles add up to angle 180°, then it ABC is a straight line, if not then ABC is not a straight line.
$61 + 55 + 63 = 179$ $179 \neq 180$

ABC is NOT a straight line

Practice questions:

Determine if ABC is a straight line in each diagram. You must show your working.

i)
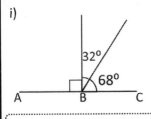

j)
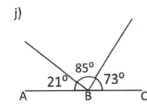

k)
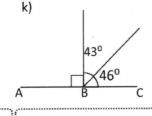

l)
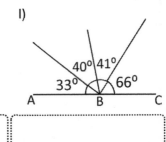

Exam question:

ACD is a triangle and ABD is a right angle.
Show that BEC is an equilateral triangle.

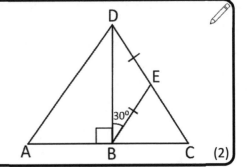

(2)

Angles in triangles

The 3 interior angles in a triangle add up to 180⁰. To find a missing angle in a triangle, add the two known angles, then subtract the answer from 180⁰.

Example
Find the missing angle: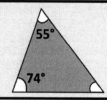

Step 1: Add 55 and 72:   55 + 72 = 127
Step 2: Subtract 127 from 180:   180 − 127 = 53

Don't forget it's angles (so needs a degree sign) **= 53°**

Practice questions:

Calculate the missing angle, x, in these triangles:

a)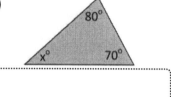

b)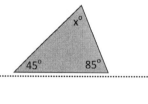

c)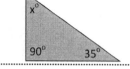

d)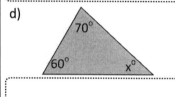

e)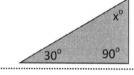

f)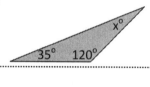

g)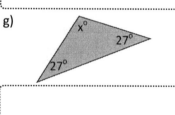

h)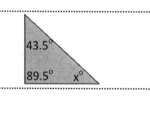

i)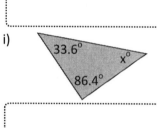

Example (notation)

Find the missing angle x

Step 1: Recognise that one angle is 90° (□ notation).
Step 2: Recognise that it is isosceles (− notation), which denotes that 2 sides and 2 angles are the same.
Step 3: 180 − 90 = 90
Step 4: 90 ÷ 2 = 45   **Answer : 45°**

Practice questions:

Calculate the missing angle, x, in these triangles:

j)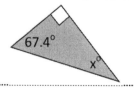

k)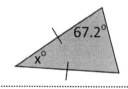

l)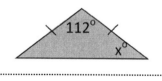

Exam question:

Calculate the value of x.

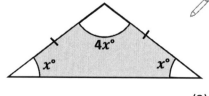

(2)

Angles in quadrilaterals

The 4 interior angles in quadrilaterals add up to 360°. To find a missing angle in a 4 sided shape, add the 3 known angles, then subtract the answer from 360°.

Examples

Find the missing angle x:

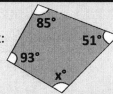

Step 1: Add 85, 93 and 51:   85 + 93 + 51 = 229
Step 2: Subtract 229 from 360:   360 − 229 = 131

Answer : 131°

Practice questions:

Calculate the missing angle, x, in these quadrilaterals:

a)

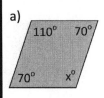

d)

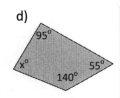

g)

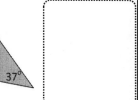

b)

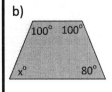

e)

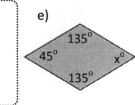

h)

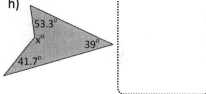

c)

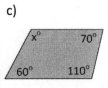

f)

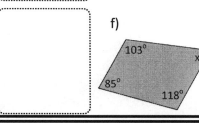

i)

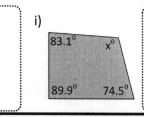

Example (notation)

Find the missing angle x and y

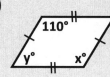

Step 1: Recognise that it's a parallelogram (/ and \\ notation).
Step 2: Know that opposite angles in parallelograms are the same.
Step 3: x = 110
Step 4: 360 − (110 + 110) = 140
Step 5: y = 140 ÷ 2 = 70   **Answer : x = 110 °, y = 70°**

Practice questions:

Calculate the missing angle, x, in these quadrilaterals:

j)

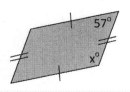

k)

l)

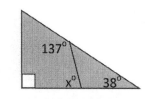

Exam question:

Calculate the value of x.

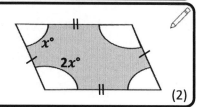

(2)

55

Congruent shapes

Congruent shapes are exactly the same. They can be rotated or reflected, but cannot be different sizes.

Examples

Which shapes are congruent to shape A?

A   B   C   D   E

Shape B
(rotated)

Shape D
(reflected)

Practice questions:

Identify the shapes which are congruent to shape A:

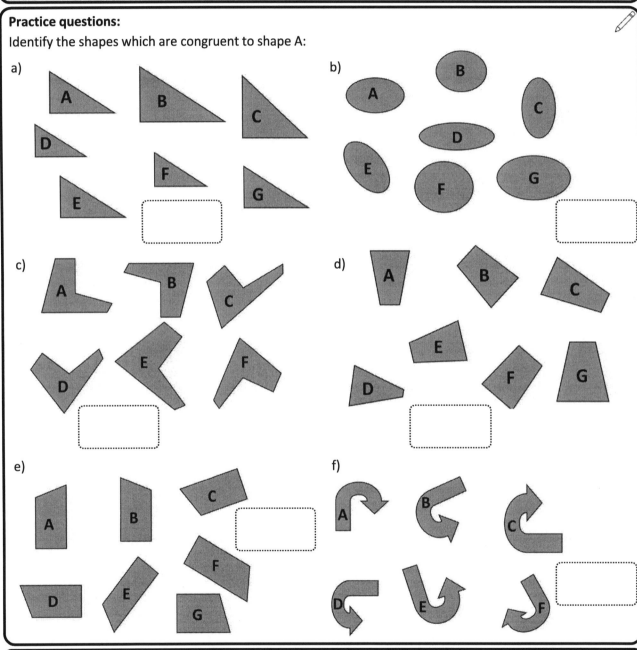

a)

b)

c)

d)

e)

f)

Exam question:

Shade one square in <u>each</u> of these two diagrams to make them congruent:

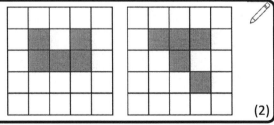

(2)

56

Lines of symmetry

A shape is symmetrical if you can draw a line through it and it is the same on both sides.
If you fold the shape along the line of symmetry, one side should fit on top of the other.

Examples: How many lines of symmetry?

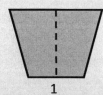
1

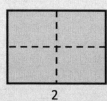
2

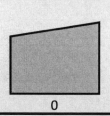
0

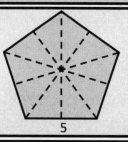
5

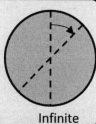
Infinite

Regular shapes (sides where all the lengths and angles are the same), such as a square and equilateral triangle have the same number of lines of symmetry as the number of their sides. So a square has 4 lines of symmetry. A circle has an infinite amount of lines of symmetry as it any diameter is a line of symmetry.

Practice questions:

How many lines of symmetry does each shape have?

a)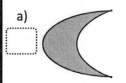

b)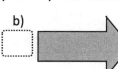

c)

d)

e)

f)

g)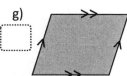

h)

i)

j)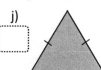

k) Shade 4 boxes so the pattern has 1 line of symmetry.

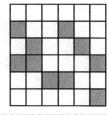

l) Shade 5 boxes so the pattern has 2 lines of symmetry.

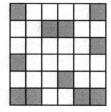

m) Shade 6 boxes so the pattern has 1 line of symmetry.

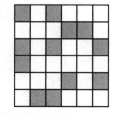

n) Shade 6 boxes so the pattern has 4 lines of symmetry.

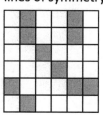

How many **planes** of symmetry do the shapes below have?

o)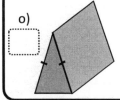

p)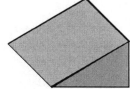

q)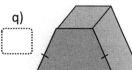

r)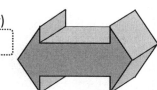

Exam question:

Shade one square in <u>each</u> of these two Diagrams so they have **only** one line of Symmetry.

a)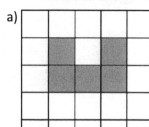

b)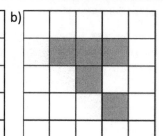

(2)

Rotational symmetry

A shape has rotational symmetry if it fits inside itself more than once when rotated around its centre. The order of rotational symmetry is the number of times the shape fits inside itself to complete a full turn.

Examples: What is the order of rotational symmetry?

 1
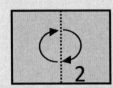 2
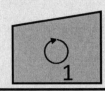 1
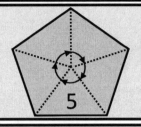 5
 ∞

Regular shapes (sides where all the lengths and angles are the same), such as a square and equilateral triangle have an order of rotational symmetry equal to the number of their sides. So a square has an order of rotational symmetry of 4. A circle has an infinite order of rotational symmetry.

Practice questions:

Write down the order of rotational symmetry of the shapes:

a)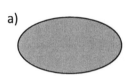

b)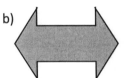

c)

d)

e)

f)

g)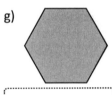

h)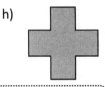

i)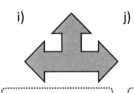

j)

k) Shade 1 box so the pattern has rotational symmetry order 2

l) Shade 1 box so the pattern has rotational symmetry order 4.

m) Shade 2 boxes so the pattern has rotational symmetry order 2.

n) Shade 2 boxes, so the pattern has rotational symmetry order 2.

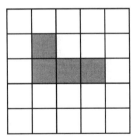
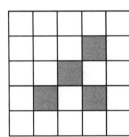
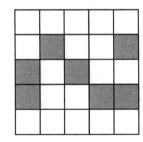
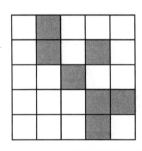

Exam question:

Shade three squares in each of these two diagrams so they have rotational symmetry order 2.

a)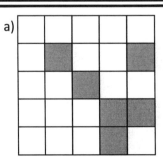

b)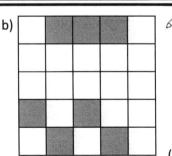

(2)

58

You need to interpret scales on a range of measuring equipment. To do this you need to work out what the scale is going up by.

Example

Write down the value on the scale marked with the arrow

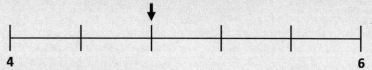

Step 1: Find the difference between the two end values: $6 - 4 = 2$

Step 2: Divide the difference by the amount of spaces on the scale (5): $2 \div 5 = 0.4$
So the scale is going up by 0.4 each time.

Step 3: Times the previous answer by the number of spaces up to the arrow and add it onto the number at the start of the scale: $4 + 2(0.4) = \mathbf{4.8}$

Practice questions:

Write down the value on the scale marked with the arrow:

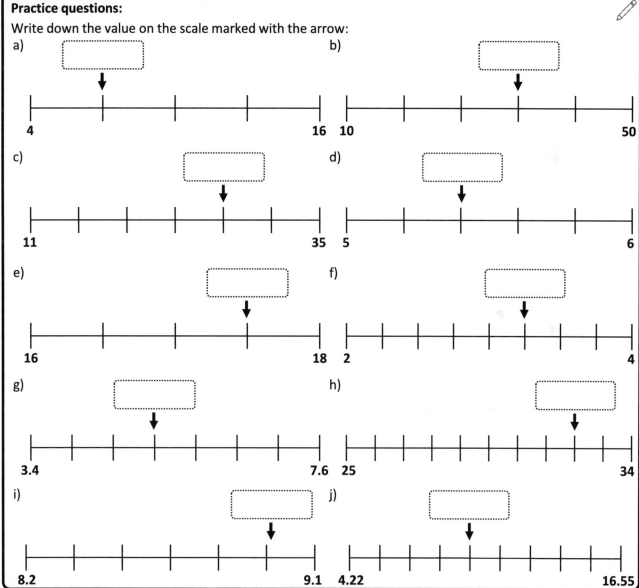

a) 4 ... 16

b) 10 ... 50

c) 11 ... 35

d) 5 ... 6

e) 16 ... 18

f) 2 ... 4

g) 3.4 ... 7.6

h) 25 ... 34

i) 8.2 ... 9.1

j) 4.22 ... 16.55

Exam question:

Write down the number represented by the arrow

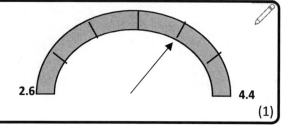

2.6 ... 4.4

(1)

Perimeter

The perimeter of a shape is the total length of the outside of a shape.
When counting squares, you have to be careful to **not** count the corners.

Examples

When counting using a square grid, make sure you count <u>the gaps</u>.

Perimeter = 12 units

Perimeter = 16 units

Practice questions:

Calculate the perimeter of the shapes by counting:

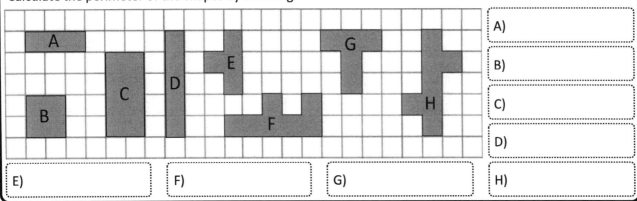

A)

B)

C)

D)

E)

F)

G)

H)

Examples

Calculate the perimeters:

To calculate the perimeter, you add up the lengths of all of the sides.

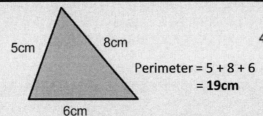

Perimeter = 5 + 8 + 6
= **19cm**

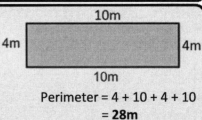

Perimeter = 4 + 10 + 4 + 10
= **28m**

Practice questions:

Calculate the perimeter of the shapes. State the units of your answer.

i)

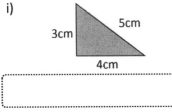

j)

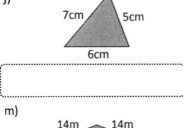

k)

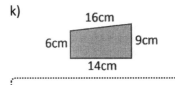

l)

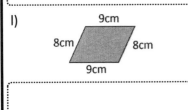

m)

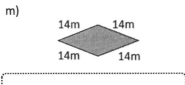

n)

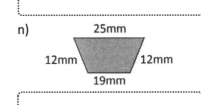

Exam question:

The perimeter of this rectangle is 14 cm.
Why is it not possible to draw a square of perimeter 14cm using whole squares on a centimetre grid?

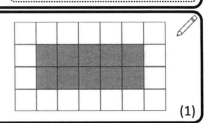

(1)

Perimeter of shapes

Sometimes when calculating the perimeter, not all the dimensions are shown. You are expected to know the properties of triangles, quadrilaterals and other regular shapes to determine lengths of missing sides.

Examples

Calculate the perimeter:

To calculate the perimeter, identify the missing sides using shape properties, and then add all the sides together.

8cm

Square

All four sides of a square are the same.

Perimeter = 8 + 8 + 8 + 8
= **32cm**

6cm

All 3 sides of an equilateral triangle are the same.

Perimeter = 6 + 6 + 6
= **18cm**

Practice questions:

Calculate the perimeter of the shapes:

a)
7mm
Square

b)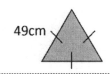
49cm

c)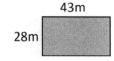
43m
28m

d)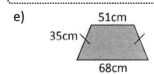
23cm
15cm

e)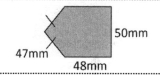
51cm
35cm
68cm

f)
50mm
47mm
48mm

Examples

Find the perimeter of the compound shape:

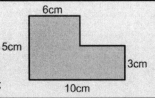
6cm
5cm
3cm
10cm

Step 1: Find lengths of missing sides
10 − 6 = 4cm
5 − 3 = 2cm

Step 2: Add all the side lengths
10 + 5 + 6 + 2 + 4 + 3 = **30cm**

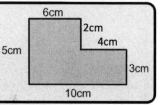
6cm
2cm
4cm
5cm
3cm
10cm

Practice questions:

Find the perimeter of the shapes:

g)
8cm
3cm
7cm
4cm

h)
5cm
11cm
6cm
6cm
8cm

i)
18cm
11cm
30cm
14cm

j)
43m
82m
53m
32m

k)
33cm
26cm
17cm
29cm
24cm

l)
45m
18m
58m
19m
21m

Exam question:

ABCD is a square. ABE is an equilateral triangle.
The perimeter of the triangle is 57cm.
Find the perimeter of the square.

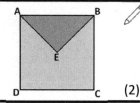
A   B
E
D   C

(2)

The area of a shape is the amount of space the shape is takes up. The units of area are mm², cm², m², km².

Examples

Find the area of the shapes shown:

You can calculate the area of a shape by counting the squares, but sometimes you have to match up parts of squares to make a whole square.

Area = 8 cm²

Area = 12 cm²

Practice questions:

Calculate the area of the shapes:

A) [ ]

B) [ ]

C) [ ]

D) [ ]   E) [ ]   F) [ ]   G) [ ]

H) [ ]

I) [ ]

J) [ ]   K) [ ]   L) [ ]   M) [ ]

N) [ ]

O) [ ]

P) [ ]   Q) [ ]   R) [ ]   S) [ ]

Exam question:

Calculate the area of the shape:

(2)

Area of rectangles

Area of a rectangle = base x height

Height | Base

Examples

Find the areas of the rectangles:

Don't forget units!

7cm | 4cm

Area = 4 x 7
= **28 m²**

4m | 11m

Area = 11 x 4 = **44m²**

Practice questions:

Calculate the area of the rectangles. State the units of your answer.

a) 3cm, 4cm

d) Square 11cm

b) 4cm, 8cm

e) 13m, 3m, 3m, 13m

c) 4cm, 7cm

f) 15m, 6m

You will sometimes have to work backwards to find a missing dimension when you are given the area.

Examples

Find the value of the missing dimensions:

3cm | Area = 21 cm² | x cm

x m | Area = 12 cm² | 6m

Area = base x height → x × 3 = 21

Area = base x height → 6 × x = 12

Don't forget units!

x = 21 ÷ 3 = **7cm**

x = 12 ÷ 6 = **2m**

Practice questions:

Calculate the value of x in the rectangles:

g) x cm, Area = 32cm², 8cm

j) 0.5cm, Area = 5cm², x cm

h) Area = 96cm², 12cm, x cm

k) x cm, 1.5cm, Area = 9cm²

i) Area = 88mm², 8mm, x mm

l) Area = 25cm², x cm, x cm

Exam question:

The area of this square and rectangle are equal. Calculate the value of x.

8cm | 16cm | x

(2)

Area of triangles

Area of a triangle = base x height ÷ 2   (Area = ½bh)

Height
Base

Examples

Find the areas of the triangles:

Don't forget units!

5cm
4cm

Area = 4 x 5 ÷ 2
= **10cm²**

4m
11m

Area = 11 x 4 ÷ 2 = **22m²**

Practice questions:

Calculate the area of the triangles. State the units of your answer.

a)
3cm
4cm

b)
4cm
6cm

c)
13cm
3cm
8cm

d)
6cm
8cm

e)
7m
10m
12m

f)
5cm
8cm
5cm

You will sometimes have to work backwards to find a missing dimension when you are given the area.

Examples

Find the value of the missing dimensions:

5cm
Area = 15cm²
b

Area = base x height ÷ 2 → b x 3 ÷ 2 = 15
b = 15 x 2 ÷ 3 = **10cm**

Don't forget units!

h
Area = 13.5cm²
9m

Area = base x height ÷ 2 → 9 x h ÷ 2 = 13.5
h = 13.5 x 2 ÷ 9 = **3m**

Practice questions:

Calculate the value of x in the triangles:

g)
7cm
Area = 35cm²
x cm

h)
x cm
Area = 12cm²
6cm

i)
2cm
Area = 10cm²
x cm

j)
3m
Area = 9m²
x m

k)
x cm
Area = 18cm²
9cm

l)
7cm
x cm
Area = 44cm²
11cm

Exam question:

Calculate the area of the triangle shown.
State the units of your answer.

20.6cm
5cm
20cm

(2)

64

Area of parallelograms

Area of a parallelogram = base x perpendicular height.
It must be the perpendicular height and **NOT the slope**.

Height | Base

Examples

Find the area of the parallelograms:

Don't forget units!

5cm

4cm

Area = 4 x 5 = **20 cm²**

3m

11m

4m

Area = 11 x 3 = **33 m²**

Practice questions:

Calculate the area of these parallelograms. State the units of your answer.

a)
4cm
6cm

b)
3cm
3cm

c)
7cm
11cm

d)
6cm
5cm
7cm

e)
7cm
6cm
9cm

f)
12cm
11cm
11cm

You will sometimes have to work backwards to find a missing dimension when you are given the area.

Examples

Find the value of the missing dimensions:

Don't forget units!

7cm
Area = 42cm²
b

Area = base x height → b x 7 = 42
b = 42 ÷ 7 = **6cm**

h
Area = 2.5m²
0.8m
5m

Area = base x height → 5 x h = 2.5
h = 2.5 ÷ 5 = **0.5m**

Practice questions:

Calculate the value of x in the parallelograms:

g)
x cm
5cm
Area = 20cm²

h)
x cm
8cm
Area = 56cm²

i)
x cm
6cm
Area = 39cm²

j)
7cm
6cm
x cm
Area = 63cm²

k)
3m
5m
x m
Area = 15.6m²

l)
2cm
0.8cm
x cm
Area = 2cm²

Exam question:

The area of this square and parallelogram are equal. Calculate the value of x.

6cm

x

8cm

(2)

Area of trapeziums

Area of a trapezium $= \frac{1}{2}(a + b)h$, where a and b are the parallel sides.

h is perpendicular distance between the two parallel sides of the trapezium.

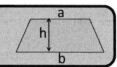

Examples

Find the areas of the trapeziums:

Don't forget units!

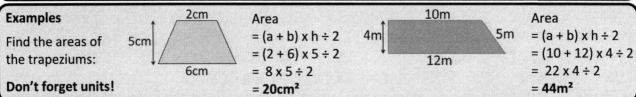

2cm / 5cm / 6cm

Area
= (a + b) x h ÷ 2
= (2 + 6) x 5 ÷ 2
= 8 x 5 ÷ 2
= **20cm²**

10m / 4m / 5m / 12m

Area
= (a + b) x h ÷ 2
= (10 + 12) x 4 ÷ 2
= 22 x 4 ÷ 2
= **44m²**

Practice questions:

Calculate the area of these trapeziums. State the units of your answer.

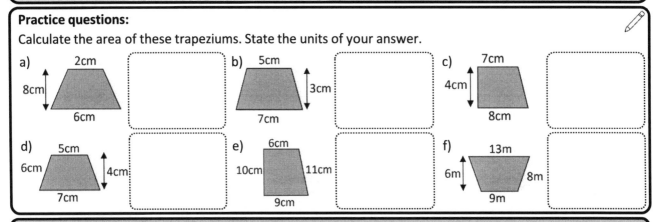

a) 2cm / 8cm / 6cm

b) 5cm / 3cm / 7cm

c) 7cm / 4cm / 8cm

d) 5cm / 6cm / 4cm / 7cm

e) 6cm / 10cm / 11cm / 9cm

f) 13m / 6m / 8m / 9m

You will sometimes have to work backwards to find a missing dimension when you are given the area.

Examples

Find the value of the missing dimensions:

Don't forget units!

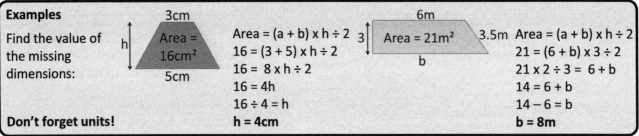

3cm / h / Area = 16cm² / 5cm

Area = (a + b) x h ÷ 2
16 = (3 + 5) x h ÷ 2
16 = 8 x h ÷ 2
16 = 4h
16 ÷ 4 = h
h = 4cm

6m / 3 / Area = 21m² / 3.5m / b

Area = (a + b) x h ÷ 2
21 = (6 + b) x 3 ÷ 2
21 x 2 ÷ 3 = 6 + b
14 = 6 + b
14 − 6 = b
b = 8m

Practice questions:

Calculate the value of x in these trapeziums.

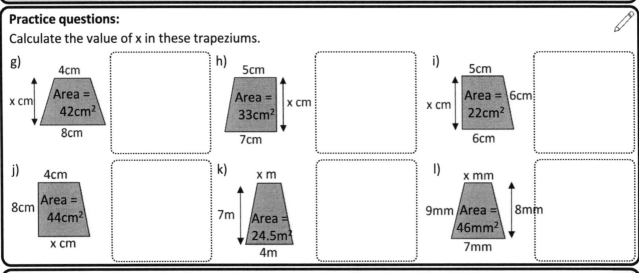

g) 4cm / x cm / Area = 42cm² / 8cm

h) 5cm / Area = 33cm² / x cm / 7cm

i) 5cm / x cm / Area = 22cm² / 6cm / 6cm

j) 4cm / 8cm / Area = 44cm² / x cm

k) x m / 7m / Area = 24.5m² / 4m

l) x mm / 9mm / Area = 46mm² / 8mm / 7mm

Exam question:

The diagram shows a rectangle which is cut into a triangle and trapezium. Some dimensions are shown.
Find the difference between the area of the dark section and the area of the light section.

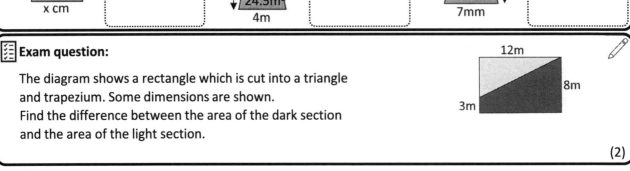

12m / 8m / 3m

(2)

Area of compound shapes (rectangles)

A compound shape is a shape made up of 2 or more simple shapes.
You need to split the shape into rectangles and then add them together.
You may need to compare opposite side lengths to find missing dimensions.

Examples

Find the area of the shape:

6cm
5cm
3cm
10cm

Step 1: Split the shape
Step 2: Find lengths of missing sides
Step 3: Area of A = 2 x 6 = 12cm²
Area of B = 3 x 10 = 30cm²
Total area = 30 + 12 = **42cm²**

(5 – 3 = 2)
6cm
A   2cm
5cm
B
10cm
3cm

Practice questions:

Calculate the total area of the compound shapes. State the units of your answer.

a)
4cm
4cm
3cm
9cm

b)
9cm
3cm
5cm
6cm

c)
3cm
5cm
7cm
4cm

d)
12m
13m
7m
6m

e)
12mm
14mm
16mm
18mm

f)
8m
4m
3m
9m

g)
13m
6m
20m
6m
7m

h)
9cm
9cm
3cm
6cm
10cm

i)
10cm
11cm
9cm   14cm   14cm
15cm   9cm
16cm

Exam question:

The diagram shows a wall with a door in it.
Calculate the area of the shaded wall.

5m
1m
4m
2m
(3)

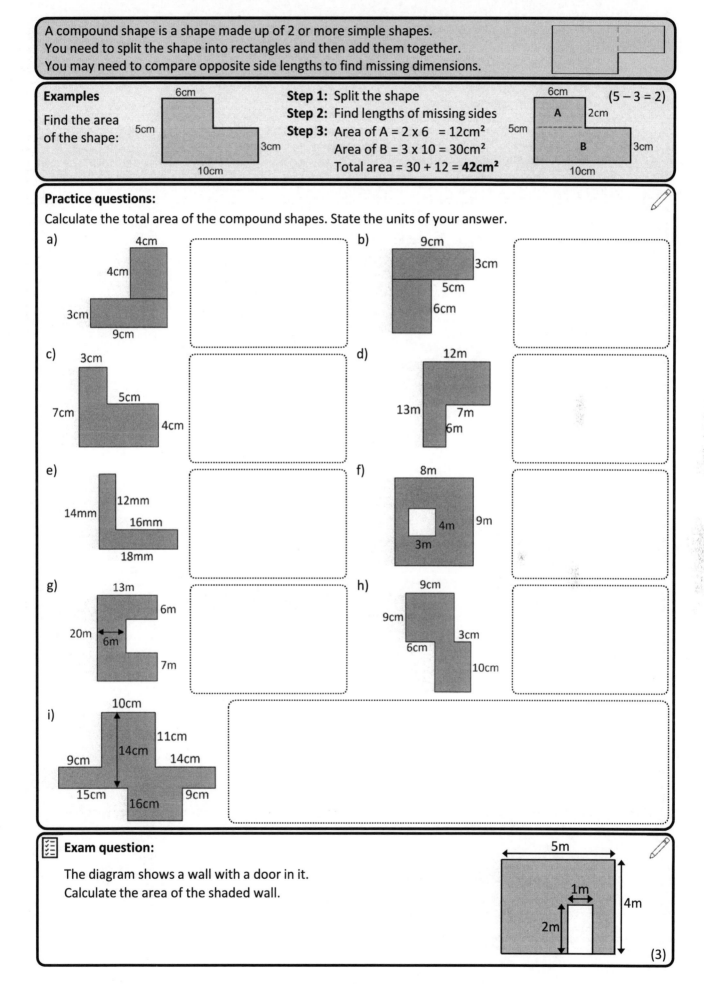

67

Area of compound shapes

A compound shape is a shape made up of 2 or more simple shapes.
You need to split the shape into shapes that you know how to work out the area of.
You may need to compare opposite sides to find missing lengths.

Examples

Find the area of the shape:

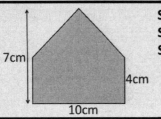

Step 1: Split the shape
Step 2: Find lengths of missing sides
Step 3: Area of A = 10 x 4 = 40cm²
Area of B = 3 x 10 ÷ 2 = 15cm²
Total area = 40 + 15 = **55cm²**

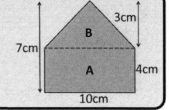

Practice questions:

Calculate the area of the compound shapes. State the units of your answer.

a)

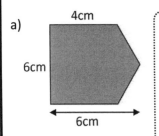

b)

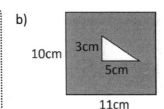

c)

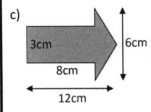

d)

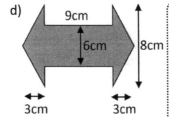

e)

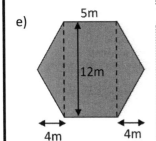

f)

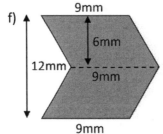

g)

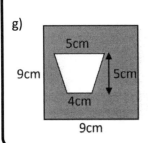

h)

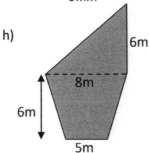

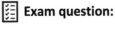

Exam question:

The diagram shows a rectangle inside a triangle.
The triangle has a base of 8m and a height of 10m.
The rectangle is 4m by 2m.
Work out the area of the shaded region.

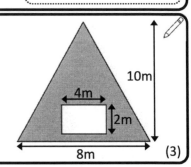

(3)

Parallel and perpendicular lines

Parallel lines are two lines which travel in the same direction. They are always the same distance apart and will never meet. Perpendicular lines meet at right angles to each other.

Examples

a) Which line is parallel to AB?   **FG – as it goes in the same direction**

b) Which line is perpendicular to AB?   **AD – as it meets at a right angle**

Practice questions:

Are the lines parallel, perpendicular or neither?

a)

b)

c)

d)

e)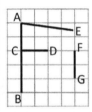

f)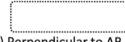

g)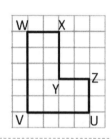

h)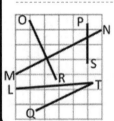

Practice questions:

Write down the line(s) which is/are:

i) Parallel to AB

j) Perpendicular to AB

k) Parallel to WX

l) Perpendicular to WX

m) Parallel to MN

n) Perpendicular to MN

o) Parallel to WX

p) Perpendicular to WX

Practice questions:

Draw a line which is :

q) Passes through C and is parallel to AB.

r) Passes through D and is perpendicular to AB.

s) Passes through O and is parallel to MN.

t) Passes through P and is perpendicular to MN.

Exam Info:

Parallel lines are not always easy to see, so in questions, to show that lines are a parallel an arrow sign is used " > ". If there are more than one set of parallel lines, more arrows are used.

This parallelogram shows how two sets or parallel sides are denoted.

Parts of a circle

You need to be familiar with the names of the different parts of a circle.

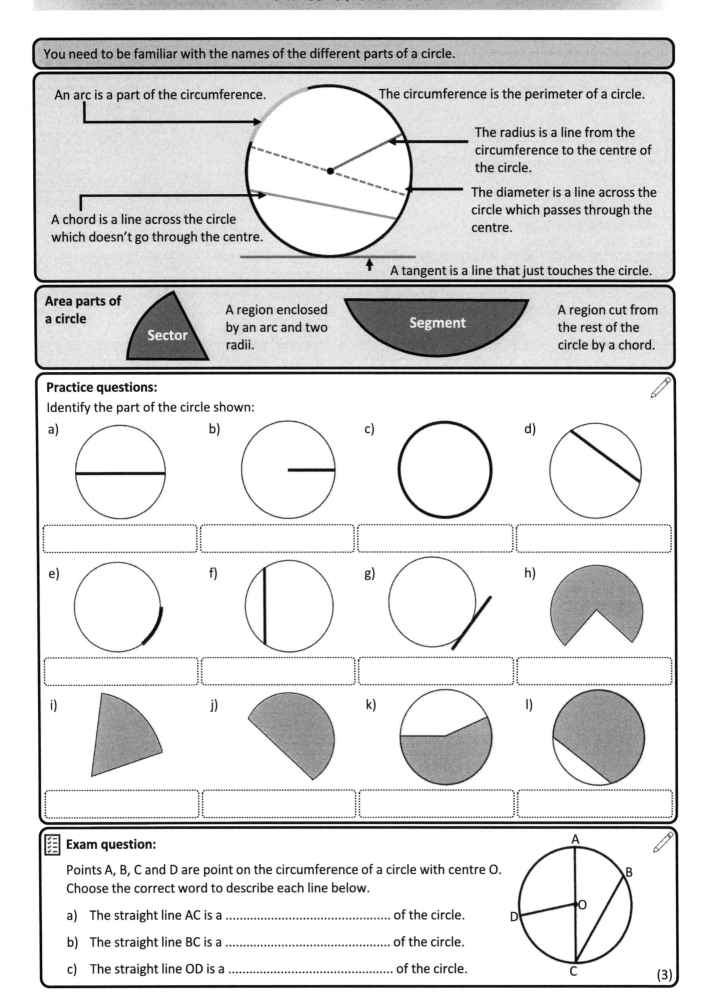

An arc is a part of the circumference.

The circumference is the perimeter of a circle.

The radius is a line from the circumference to the centre of the circle.

The diameter is a line across the circle which passes through the centre.

A chord is a line across the circle which doesn't go through the centre.

A tangent is a line that just touches the circle.

Area parts of a circle

Sector — A region enclosed by an arc and two radii.

Segment — A region cut from the rest of the circle by a chord.

Practice questions:

Identify the part of the circle shown:

a)

b)

c)

d)

e)

f)

g)

h)

i)

j)

k)

l)

Exam question:

Points A, B, C and D are point on the circumference of a circle with centre O. Choose the correct word to describe each line below.

a) The straight line AC is a .... of the circle.

b) The straight line BC is a .... of the circle.

c) The straight line OD is a .... of the circle.

(3)

3D shapes

You need to be familiar with the names of the different 3D shapes.

| Cube | Cuboid | Cylinder | Sphere | Cone | Triangular Prism | Pyramid |

A **face** is a flat or curved surface on a 3D shape.   An **edge** is the line where two faces meet.
A **Vertex** is a corner where two edges meet – the plural is **vertices**.

Example

What is the name of the shape?   **Cuboid**
How many vertices?   Count the corners   **8**
How many edges?   Count the lines between faces   **12**
How many faces?   Count the surfaces   **6**

Practice questions:

Fill in the boxes for each 3D shape:

a)   Name: [＿＿＿＿＿＿＿]   Number of faces: [＿＿＿＿＿]
     Number of vertices: [＿＿＿＿]   Number of edges: [＿＿＿＿]

b)   Name: [＿＿＿＿＿＿＿]   Number of faces: [＿＿＿＿＿]
     Number of vertices: [＿＿＿＿]   Number of edges: [＿＿＿＿]

c)   Name: [＿＿＿＿＿＿＿]   Number of faces: [＿＿＿＿＿]
     Number of vertices: [＿＿＿＿]   Number of edges: [＿＿＿＿]

d)   Name: [＿＿＿＿＿＿＿]   Number of faces: [＿＿＿＿＿]
     Number of vertices: [＿＿＿＿]   Number of edges: [＿＿＿＿]

e)   Name: [＿＿＿＿＿＿＿]   Number of faces: [＿＿＿＿＿]
     Number of vertices: [＿＿＿＿]   Number of edges: [＿＿＿＿]

f)   Name: [＿＿＿＿＿＿＿]   Number of faces: [＿＿＿＿＿]
     Number of vertices: [＿＿＿＿]   Number of edges: [＿＿＿＿]

g)   Name: [＿＿＿＿＿＿＿]   Number of faces: [＿＿＿＿＿]
     Number of vertices: [＿＿＿＿]   Number of edges: [＿＿＿＿]

Drawing Bar charts

A bar chart is a graph where the height of the bar represents the frequency.

A bar chart must have:
- Bars of the same width
- Equal gaps between the bars
- Fully labelled axis
- Frequency on the y-axis

Example

The table shows data on 30 peoples favourite colours. Draw a bar chart to represent the data.

Colour	Frequency
Blue	9
Green	2
Red	7
Pink	12

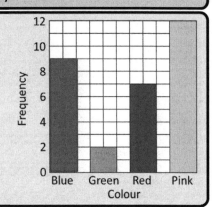

Practice questions:

Draw a bar chart to represent the data:

a)

Travel	Frequency
Train	8
Car	12
Walk	6

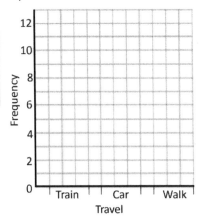

b)

Fruit	Frequency
Lime	2
Banana	7
Orange	5
Mango	11

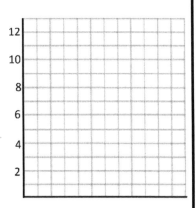

c)

Colour	Frequency
Green	13
Yellow	5
Pink	16
Blue	9

d)

Pet	Frequency
Dog	17
Cat	14
Budgie	2
Ferret	6

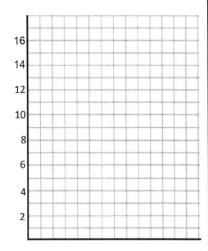

Exam question:

A hardware store sells a variety of materials.

The store sells twice as much wood as slate and twice as much marble as granite.

It sells 45m² altogether, complete the bar chart.

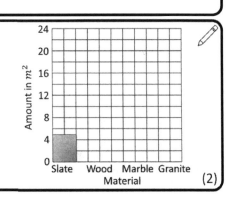

(2)

When interpreting bar charts, remember that the height of the bar is the frequency.

Example

The bar chart shows information on peoples favourite fruit:

a) Which fruit was most popular?

The bar with the highest frequency (tallest bar): **Mango**

b) How many people liked pears best?

Read the height of the bar labelled pear: **16**

c) How many more people preferred mangos to bananas?

Find the two heights and find the difference:

Mangos = 22 and Bananas = 17 → 22 − 17 = **5**

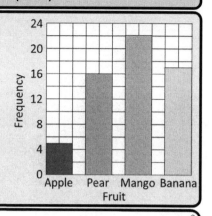

Practice questions:

From the bar chart, how many:

a) People have green eyes?

b) People are there altogether?

c) More people have blue eyes than green eyes?

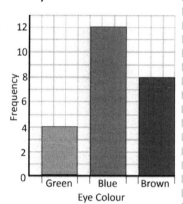

From the bar chart, how many:

d) People like pizza?

e) People are there altogether?

f) More people prefer curry to burger?

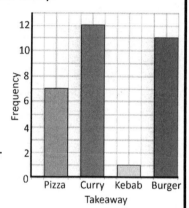

From the bar chart, how many:

g) Coffees were sold on Monday?

h) Coffees were sold altogether?

i) More coffees were sold on Friday, than Monday?

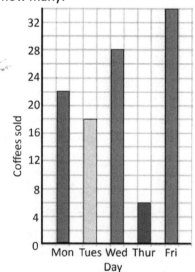

From the bar chart:

j) What was the temperature on Friday?

k) Which day had the highest temperature?

l) What was the range in temperatures?

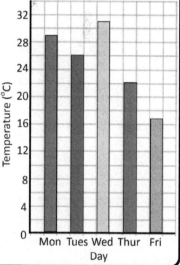

Exam question:

A shop sells fruit and records their sales in the bar chart.

a) How many apples **and** pears were sold altogether?

b) How many more mangos were sold than bananas?

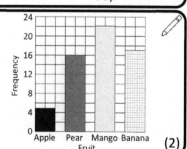

(2)

A dual bar chart is used to compare data between different groups. It is drawn like a normal bar chart but with side by side bars for each category. A key must be included so the graph makes sense.

The same rules apply to dual bar charts as they did to bar charts.

Example

The table shows data on boys and girls favourite colours.
Draw a dual bar chart to represent the data.

Colour	Boys	Girls
Blue	7	8
Green	10	1
Red	2	5
Pink	6	11

Remember to include a Key!

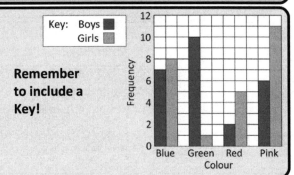

Practice questions:

Draw a dual bar chart to represent the data:

a)

Eye	Female	Male
Green	8	12
Brown	11	4
Blue	4	7

Key:

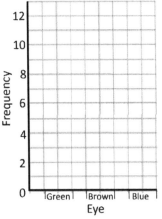

b)

Animal	Under 25	Over 25
Panda	10	8
Koala	11	4
Zebra	2	7
Lion	8	12

Key:

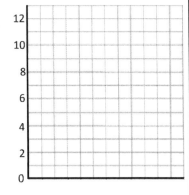

c)

Fruit	Male	Female
Lychee	4	2
Melon	8	5
Kiwi	15	12
Cherry	9	17

Key:

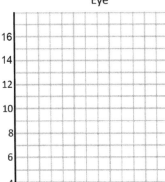

d)

Drink	Under 50	Over 50
Cola	18	12
Energy	14	4
Water	11	15
Orange	8	17

Key:

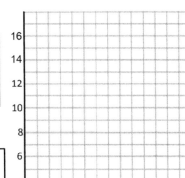

Exam question:

Adults & children were asked what sports they enjoyed.
The table shows the results.
Draw a dual bar chart to represent this information.

	Football	Running	Swimming
Adults	4	5	3
Children	3	7	6

Key:

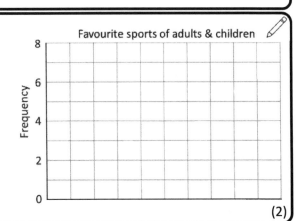

Favourite sports of adults & children

(2)

When interpreting bar charts remember that the height of the bar is the frequency.

Example

The chart shows data on peoples favourite fruit.

Key: Boys ▰ Girls ▱

a) Which fruit did girls prefer?
   The fruit with the highest frequency (tallest bar): **Banana**

b) How many people liked pears best?
   Read the height of bars labelled pear and add: 14 + 7 = **21**

c) How many more boys preferred mangos to girls?
   Find the two heights and find the difference:
   Boys = 22 and Girls = 13   →   22 − 13 = **9**

Practice questions:

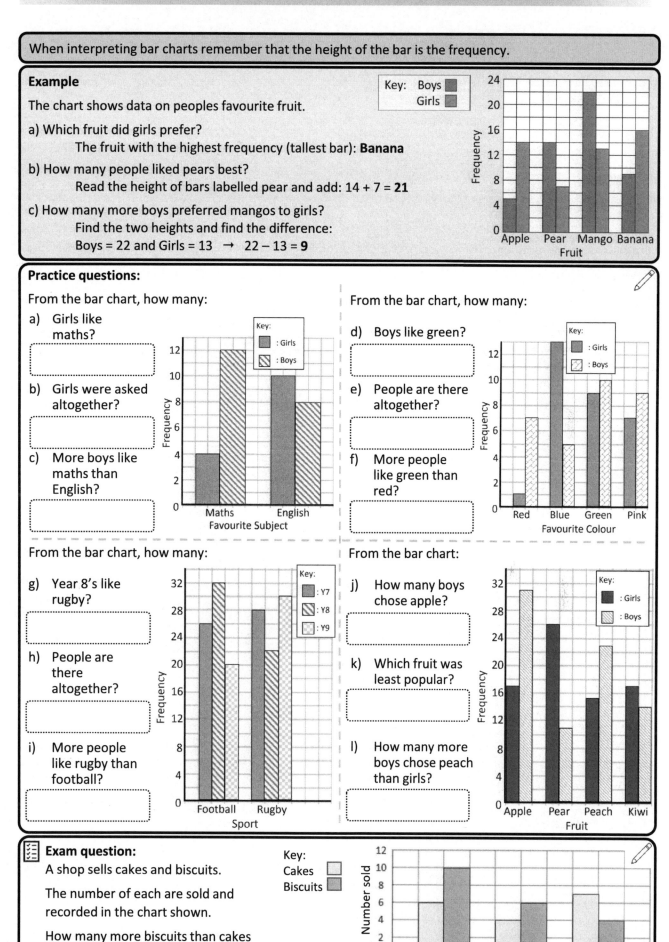

From the bar chart, how many:

a) Girls like maths?

b) Girls were asked altogether?

c) More boys like maths than English?

From the bar chart, how many:

d) Boys like green?

e) People are there altogether?

f) More people like green than red?

From the bar chart, how many:

g) Year 8's like rugby?

h) People are there altogether?

i) More people like rugby than football?

From the bar chart:

j) How many boys chose apple?

k) Which fruit was least popular?

l) How many more boys chose peach than girls?

Exam question:

A shop sells cakes and biscuits.

The number of each are sold and recorded in the chart shown.

How many more biscuits than cakes were sold over the three days?

Key:
Cakes ▯
Biscuits ▦

(2)

75

Drawing pictograms

A pictogram is a graph which displays information using pictures. You must include a key to be able to understand the pictogram. Pictogram shapes must be easily interpreted and sizes must be consistent.

Example

The table shows how many goals each person scored in the season. Complete the pictogram:

Name	Number of Goals
Claire	8
Sally	2
Fay	7
Betty	14

Choose a shape to represent goals

Claire: 8 goals = 4 footballs

Sally: 2 goals = 1 football

Fay: 7 goals = 3 ½ footballs

Betty: 14 goals = 7 footballs

Key: 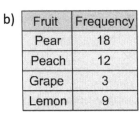 = 2 goals

Claire	⚽⚽⚽⚽
Sally	⚽
Fay	⚽⚽⚽◖
Betty	⚽⚽⚽⚽⚽⚽⚽

Practice questions:

Use the tables to fill in the pictograms:

a)

Hair	Frequency
Blonde	10
Brown	4
Black	8
Ginger	2

Key : ■ = 2 people

Blonde	
Brown	
Black	
Ginger	

b)

Fruit	Frequency
Pear	18
Peach	12
Grape	3
Lemon	9

Key : ● = 3 people

Pear	
Peach	
Grape	
Lemon	

c)

Colour	Frequency
Blue	6
Orange	3
Red	9
Grey	8

Key : ▼ = 2 people

Blue	
Orange	
Red	
Grey	

d)

Animal	Frequency
Cow	16
Pig	2
Goat	20
Sheep	30

Key : ■ = 8 people

Cow	
Pig	
Goat	
Sheep	

e)

Meat	Frequency
Chicken	12
Lamb	7
Beef	10
Pork	3

Key : ▲ = 2 people

Chicken	
Lamb	
Beef	
Pork	

f)

Team	Frequency
Chelsea	9
Arsenal	12
Leeds	19
Millwall	2

Key : ● = 4 people

Chelsea	
Arsenal	
Leeds	
Millwall	

g)

Capital	Frequency
Rome	10
Paris	16
Lima	2
Athens	14

Key : ▲ = 4 people

Rome	
Paris	
Lima	
Athens	

h)

Herb	Frequency
Thyme	26
Mint	16
Dill	38
Parsley	44

Key : ■ = 8 people

Thyme	
Mint	
Dill	
Parsley	

Exam question:

The table shows the number of cars sold by a garage over the course of a week.

a) Complete the pictogram of this data.

(Monday has been completed)

	Frequency
Monday	9
Tuesday	13
Wednesday	11
Thursday	11
Friday	9

Monday	$ $ $ $ ¢
Tuesday	
Wednesday	
Thursday	
Friday	

Key: $ = 2 car sales

(2)

When reading/interpreting pictograms , you must read and/or identify the key carefully. All content and questions will be related to the key which is either provided or needs to be found.

Example

The pictogram shows the number of drinks sold at a cafe.

Tea	
Coffee	
Hot Chocolate	
Milkshake	

Key : ☐ = 4 drinks

a) Which drink was most popular?

Coffee - because it has the most boxes.

b) How many hot chocolates were sold?

4 + 4 + 2(half a full square) = **10**

c) How many more people bought a tea than a milkshake?

Tea = 5 x 4 = 20, Milkshake = 3.75 x 4 = 15   20 – 15 = **5 more people**

Practice questions:

Using the pictograms provided to answer the questions.

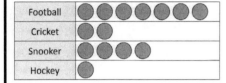

Key:
⬤ = 3 people

a) How many people like cricket?

b) How many people like snooker?

c) How many people are there altogether?

d) How many more people like football than cricket?

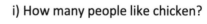
Key:
🥤 = 2 people

e) How many people like chocolate?

f) How many people like bubble-gum?

g) How many people are there altogether?

h) How many more people like vanilla than strawberry?

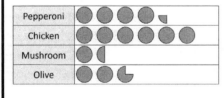

Key:
⬤ = 8 people

i) How many people like chicken?

j) How many people like olive?

k) How many people are there altogether?

l) How many more people like pepperoni than mushroom?

Exam question:

The pictogram shows the number of strikes that a team scored in a game of ten pin bowling.

a) If Trevor got 6 strikes complete the Key.

b) How many more strikes did Bob get than Carl?

Carl	🎳🎳🎳
Bob	🎳🎳🎳🎳
Trevor	🎳🎳🎳
Paul	🎳

Key: 🎳 = _____ Strikes

(2)

A frequency table is used to record data. A tally can be kept to make it easier to calculate the frequency.

Example

20 people recorded their shoe sizes, the results are shown below:

3, 5, 6, 4, 8, 6, 6, 5, 3, 8, 6, 4, 6, 3, 6, 5, 5, 4, 5, 6

The first row (headings) describes the data.

All the different data values should be put in (**Shoe size**).

The second column is for the tally.

The final column is for the frequency.

卌 - is 5 in a tally chart.

SHOE SIZE	TALLY	FREQUENCY
3	III	3
4	III	3
5	卌	5
6	卌 II	7
7		0
8	II	2

Practice questions:

Calculate the frequencies from the tally charts given in these tables:

a)

Hair Colour	Tally	Frequency
Brown	卌 卌 II	
Black	III	
Blonde	卌 IIII	
Other	卌 I	

b)

Shoe Size	Tally	Frequency
5	卌 卌 卌	
6	卌 卌 I	
7		
8	IIII	

c) Record the eye colours in the table:

Green, Blue, Brown, Brown, Brown,
Blue, Brown, Green, Brown, Green,
Brown, Brown, Brown, Blue, Brown,
Green, Brown, Green, Blue, Blue,
Brown, Brown, Blue, Green, Blue,
Brown, Brown, Green, Brown, Blue

Eye Colour	Tally	Frequency
Green		
Blue		
Brown		

d) Record the number of goals in the table:

1, 0, 2, 0, 1, 2, 0, 3, 1, 2,
4, 1, 1, 0, 2, 1, 3, 1, 3, 4,
1, 2, 4, 1, 5, 0, 2, 1, 3, 1,
3, 2, 1, 0, 2, 0, 1, 2, 5, 3,
2, 1, 3, 1, 3, 2, 1, 0, 2, 0,
5, 2, 0, 3, 0, 2, 1, 3, 1, 2

Goals	Tally	Frequency

Exam question:

Steve collected 21 plants and wrote down the lengths of their leaves, to the nearest cm. Here are his results:

5, 5, 6, 4, 2, 8, 5, 5, 7, 6, 7, 4, 5, 3, 4, 4, 6, 7, 5, 8, 7

Complete the frequency table to show Steve's results.

Length in cm	Tally	Frequency
2		
3		
4		
5		
6		
7		
8		

(2)

Continuous data can be **grouped** in a frequency table. Inequalities can be used to avoid overlaps of the data.

Example

10 people recorded their heights in cm:

172.3, 168.7, 180.5, 175, 177.8, 166.6, 180, 164.9, 178.6, 179

You must ensure the groups don't overlap.

The 3rd group for example includes 175, but the 4th group does not.

≤ means less than or equal to.

HEIGHT	TALLY	FREQUENCY
160 < X ≤ 165	I	1
165 < X ≤ 170	II	2
170 < X ≤ 175	II	2
175 < X ≤ 180	IIII	4
180 < X ≤ 185	I	1

Practice questions:

a) Record the shoes sizes in the grouped frequency table provided:

3, 6, 4, 7, 1, 6, 5, 3, 8, 3, 2, 8, 5, 8
7, 4, 2, 6, 5, 7, 4, 6, 8, 3, 6, 5, 6, 5

Shoe Size	Tally	Frequency
1 - 2		
3 - 4		
5 - 6		
7 - 8		

b) Record the ages in the grouped frequency table provided:

25, 53, 44, 30, 36, 44, 18, 8, 22, 40,
25, 18, 55, 31, 15, 29, 50, 9, 54, 10
46, 17, 20, 44, 52, 39, 50, 14, 16, 3

Age	Tally	Frequency
0 < a ≤ 10		
10 < a ≤ 20		
20 < a ≤ 30		
30 < a ≤ 40		
40 < a ≤ 50		
50 < a ≤ 60		

c) Record the heights in the grouped frequency table provided:

156.3, 166.7, 170, 158, 184.8, 160,
175.2, 179.9, 166, 174.8, 159.3, 166,
180, 166.2, 171, 175, 174.8, 183,
168.7, 173.7, 166, 181, 165, 177.3

Height	Tally	Frequency
155 < h ≤ 160		
160 < h ≤ 165		
165 < h ≤ 170		
170 < h ≤ 175		
175 < h ≤ 180		
180 < h ≤ 185		

Exam question:

Steve collected 16 plants and wrote down the heights in cm. Here are his results:

35, 38, 8, 39, 22, 24, 27, 31, 40, 27, 42, 29, 21, 37, 58, 66

Complete the grouped frequency table to show Steve's results.

Height	Tally	Frequency
0 < a ≤ 20		
20 < a ≤ 40		
40 < a ≤ 60		
60 < a ≤ 80		

(3)

Median

The median is the middle value, once all the data has been placed in numerical order (usually ascending). If you have two numbers in the middle, you can add them together and divide by two to find the median.

Example: With an <u>odd</u> set of numbers

Find the median of the data: 3, 7, 5, 9, 2, 6, 5   (**odd** set of data – 7 numbers)
Step 1: Put the numbers in order from smallest to largest : 2, 3, 5, 5, 6, 7, 9
Step 2: Cross off the numbers from both ends one by one : 2̸, 3̸, 5̸, 5, 6̸, 7̸, 9̸
Step 3: The **median** is the value that is left in the middle.   **Median = 5**

Practice questions:

Find the median of each of these data sets:

a) 14, 17, 19, 8, 9, 1, 5

b) 7, 15, 20, 11, 19

c) 7, 8, 3, 8, 7, 6, 8, 2, 5

d) 3, 7, 12, 4, 2, 9, 5, 3, 7

e) 52, 25, 61, 19, 24

f) 4.8, 8.1, 2.2, 1.9, 7.1

Example: With an <u>even</u> set of numbers

Find the median of the data: 6, 9, 2, 0, 4, 8   (**even** set of data – 6 numbers)
Step 1: Put the numbers in order from smallest to largest : 0, 2, 4, 6, 8, 9
Step 2: Cross off the numbers from both ends one by one : 0̸, 2̸, 4, 6, 8̸, 9̸
Step 3: With an even set of data, you will be left with 2 values in the middle, so you need to find the "half-way" point between the 2 values given. You can do this by adding the two values together, then divide by 2.
Median = (4 + 6) ÷ 2 = 10 ÷ 2 = **5**

Practice questions:

Find the median of each of these data sets:

g) 3, 7, 3, 4, 6, 8

h) 9, 3, 5, 10, 13, 1

i) 2, 0, 8, 4, 4, 6, 3, 8

j) 8, 9, 7, 6, 3, 1, 0, 7

k) 6.2, 8.6, 2.2, 4.6

l) 8.5, 1.5, 0.5, 2.4, 9.4, 4.6

Exam question:

Colin rolled a 6-sided dice 8 times.
Here are his scores: **3, 5, 4, 6, 3, 2, 1, 6**
Work out the median of Colins scores.

(1)

Mode and Range

The mode is the value that occurs the most times in a set of data. There can be more than one mode and if there is no value that occurs more than any other (all unique data), then there is **no** mode.

Examples
Identify the mode(s) of each set of data:

④ 7, 5, ④ 2, 6, 5, ④   4 appears the most times   **Mode = 4**

⑨ 13, ② 7, ⑨ 4, ②   2 & 9 appear the most times   **Mode = 2 & 9**

8, 1, 7, 9, 13, 4, 6   No number appears the most   **No Mode**

Practice questions:

Find the mode(s) of each of these data sets:

a) 8, 11, 8, 4, 7

b) 12, 6, 12, 6, 12, 7

c) 4, 7, 4, 14, 7, 7

d) 6, 3, 6, 9, 3, 8, 6

e) 13, 13, 19, 11, 42, 9

f) 8, 3, 5, 2, 4, 3, 5, 7

g) 7, 2, 1, 2, 3, 1, 2, 4, 1

h) 8, 12, 14, 9, 7, 4, 13, 12

i) 14, 4, 7, 9, 24, 8, 17, 2

j) 6, -6, 2, 2, -1

k) 4, -4, -7, -2, 7, 5

l) -15, 8, -13, -13, -31, 31

The range is the difference between the highest number and the lowest number. It can easily be calculated by subtracting the smallest value away from the biggest value. Range = highest value − smallest value.

Examples:
Calculate the ranges of each set of data:

3, 7, 5, ⑨ ② 6, 5, 4   **Range** = 9 − 2 = **7**

Highest number = 9   Lowest number = 2

9, ④ ⑯ 8, 11, 9, 12, 5   **Range** = 16 − 4 = **12**

Highest number = 16   Lowest number = 4

Practice questions:

Find the range of each of these data sets:

m) 14, 17, 19, 8, 9, 1, 5

n) 7, 15, 20, 11, 19, 14

o) 7, 13, 3, 4, 7, 6, 9, 2, 5

p) 1, 7, 12, 4, 2, 9, 5, 3, 7

q) 51, 25, 61, 19, 24, 18

r) 13, 17, 14, 8, 9, 1, 5

s) 7, 15, 20, 11, 19, 42

t) 7, 8, -3, 7, 6, 8, -1, 5

u) 2, -4, -7, -2, 7, 8

v) -15, 8, -13, -15, -31, 31

Exam question:

Colin rolled a 6-sided dice 12 times.

Here are his scores: **6, 3, 5, 4, 6, 3, 2, 1, 6, 4, 2, 1**

a) Work out the mode of his scores.

b) Work out the range of his scores.

(1)

Mean

To calculate the mean you need to add up the values and then divide the total by how many values there are.

Examples:

Calculate the mean of each set of data:

a) 2, 6, 5, 7

Step 1: Add the numbers together: 2 + 6 + 5 + 7 = 20
Step 2: Count the number of values: 4
Step 3: Mean = 20 ÷ 4 = **5**

b) 5, 7, 2, 12, 8, 5, 4, 9, 4, 1

Step 1: Add the numbers together: 57
Step 2: Count the number of values: 10
Step 3: Mean = 57 ÷ 10 = **5.7**

Practice questions:

Find the mean of each of these data sets.   (Leave you answer to 2 decimal places)

a) 3, 6, 6, 5

b) 5, 3, 8, 4

c) 2, 9, 8, 6, 8, 3

d) 7, 5, 10, 9, 9

e) 1, 17, 3, 6, 12, 9

f) 52, 25, 61, 19, 24

g) 71, 81, 34, 88, 27, 56, 13

h) 53, 96, 75, 12, 73, 52

i) 8.2, 7.1, 5.4, 9.9

j) 3.2, 8.5, 4.1, 7.8, 9.2

k) -8, 6, 5, 9, -1

l) -8, -7, -1, 0, -2, -8

m) The advertised temperature for a holiday resort is found by taking the mean over 8 days during July and August. What should the advertised temperature be if the readings (in °c) were: 12, 18, 9, 12, 15, 20, 21, 13.

n) The advertised temperature for a holiday resort is found by taking the mean over 11 days during July and August. What should the advertised temperature be, to the nearest degree, if the readings (in °c) were: 25, 32, 31, 28, 36, 28, 35.

Exam question:

8 boys and 8 girls from a class run 200m.

The times taken, to the nearest second, for each girl are: 30, 40, 48, 36, 38, 42, 52, 58

The mean of the boys times is 48 seconds.

Thomas says that "on average, the boys in our class are faster than the girls." Is he correct?

(2)

Two-way tables

A two way table is used to show the relationship between two variables.
One category goes along the top and the other is shown down the side.

Example

The two way table shows information on gender and eye colour.

	Blue	Green	Brown
Male	13	9	19
Female	14	4	21

a) How many males have green eyes? **9**

b) How many females are there? 14 + 4 + 21 = **39**

c) How many people have brown eyes? 19 + 21 = **40**

d) How many people are there altogether? 13 + 9 + 19 + 14 + 4 + 21 = **80**

Practice questions:

a) How many girls have brown eyes? [ ]

b) How many boys don't have brown eyes? [ ]

c) How many girls are there? [ ]

d) How many people have brown eyes? [ ]

e) How many people are there altogether? [ ]

	Brown Eyes	Not Brown Eyes	Total
Girls	15	8	23
Boys	7	14	21
Total	22	22	44

f) How many under 21s like Rock? [ ]

g) How many over 21s like Dance? [ ]

h) How many people like Rock? [ ]

i) How many people are there altogether? [ ]

	Pop	Rock	Dance	Total
Under 21	12	6	19	
Over 21	7	13	14	
Total				

j) How many over 40s like Pizza? [ ]

k) How many under 30s like Curry? [ ]

l) How many people like Curry? [ ]

m) How many over 40s are there? [ ]

n) How many people are there altogether? [ ]

	Pizza	Curry	Fish & Chips
Under 30	41	23	9
Between 30 and 40	32	33	18
Over 40	18	6	32

Exam question:

The two-way table shows the favourite subjects of students in each year group.

	English	Maths	Science
Year 9	47	62	58
Year 10	58	57	55
Year 11	59	42	64

a) How many students' favourite subject was Maths?

b) How many more students preferred Science to English?

(2)

83

Completing two-way tables

You will usually be asked to fill in the missing values in a two way table.

Example

Complete the two way table

	Football	Tennis	Rugby	Total
Male		8		
Female			4	28
Total	23	18		50

Male total: $50 - 28 = 22$

Rugby total: $50 - 23 - 18 = 9$

Female tennis: $18 - 8 = 10$

Male football: $22 - 8 - 5 = 9$

Female football: $28 - 10 - 4 = 14$

Male rugby: $9 - 4 = 5$

	Football	Tennis	Rugby	Total
Male	9	8	5	22
Female	14	10	4	28
Total	23	18	9	50

HINT : Each row and column must total – so check at the end.

Practice questions:

Complete the two way tables:

a)

	Brown hair	Not brown hair	Total
Female	9		
Male			13
Total	18		30

b)

	French	German	Total
Female	14		
Male		6	24
Total		19	

c)

	Green	Blue	Brown	Total
Under 12	14		6	27
Over 12		8		
Total			18	50

d)

	Bread	Pasta	Rice	Total
Girl			27	63
Boy	18	23		
Total	36		42	

e) People were asked if they liked cats or dogs. Complete the two-way tables using the following information:
- 24 males were asked
- 27 people like dogs
- 12 females like cats
- 13 males like dogs

	Cat	Dog	Total
Male			
Female			
Total			

f) People were asked which sport they preferred. Complete the two-way tables using the following information:
- 80 people were asked
- 36 people were over 20
- 18 people chose rugby
- 21 over 20s chose football
- 7 under 20s chose rugby
- 12 under 20s chose tennis

	Football	Rugby	Tennis	Total
Under 20				
Over 20				
Total				

Exam question:

The two-way table shows the favourite subjects of a year group

a) Complete the two way table

b) How many students favourite subject was Art?

	Art	Cooking	Music	Total
Girl			16	45
Boy	12	19		
Total		32		94

(3)

Probabilities from two-way tables

You must read the question carefully when calculating probabilities from two-way tables.

Example

From information given in the two-way table, what is the probability:

a) A person picked at random is female?

28 females, 50 people in total → $\frac{28}{50}$

b) A person picked at random prefers tennis?

18 tennis, 50 people in total → $\frac{18}{50}$

c) A male picked at random prefers rugby?

5 rugby males, 22 males in total → $\frac{5}{22}$

d) A female picked at random prefers football?

14 football females, 28 females in total → $\frac{14}{28}$

	Football	Tennis	Rugby	Total
Male	9	8	5	22
Female	14	10	4	28
Total	23	18	9	50

HINT: When told that you have selected a male, the probability needs to reflect this, so you just need to concentrate on the top lines values.

Practice questions:

Use the two-way tables to answer.

	Blue Eyes	Not Blue Eyes	Total
Girls	2	7	9
Boys	5	6	11
Total	7	13	20

a) I pick a person at random, calculate the probability that they have blue eyes.

b) I pick a person at random, calculate the probability that they are a girl.

c) I pick a boy at random, calculate the probability they don't have blue eyes.

	Jazz	Rap	Hip Hop	Total
Under 18	3	10	13	
Over 18	5	11	8	
Total				

d) I pick a person at random, calculate the probability that they like hip hop.

e) I pick a person at random, calculate the probability that they like jazz.

f) I pick an over 18 at random, calculate the probability that like rap music

	Brown	Ketchup	BBQ
Under 50	8	12	14
Between 50 and 65	12	14	9
Over 65	15	13	3

g) I pick a person at random, calculate the probability that they prefer brown sauce.

h) I pick a person at random, calculate the probability that they are 50 or over.

i) I pick an under 50 at random, calculate the probability that they prefer BBQ sauce.

Exam question:

The two-way table shows the favourite subjects of 3 year groups.

a) A random student is picked, what is the probability they are from year 7?

b) A year 9 student was chosen at random, what is the probability their favourite subject was maths?

	Maths	English	Science	Total
Y7	13	24	9	46
Y8	23	19	9	51
Y9	3	21	29	53
Total	39	64	47	150

(3)

Pie charts

A pie chart is a circular graph where the data is represented by sectors. Each sector represents a proportion, **not** an amount. If you are given an amount of people, you may be able to calculate values of each sector.

Example:

The pie chart shows how 40 pupils in year 8 travel to school:

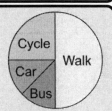

a) What is the most popular method of travel? **Walking**

b) How many people cycle to school? The sector is a quarter of the circle. 40 ÷ 4 = 10
So **10** people cycle to school.

c) Half of the people in year 9 catch the bus. In which year do the most students catch the bus? You cannot tell because the pie chart shows the proportion not the amount; you don't know how many year 9's were asked

Practice questions:

The pie chart shows the eye colour of 20 people.

a) Which was the most popular eye colour?

b) What is the least popular eye colour?

c) How many people have brown eyes?

d) If 6 people have blue eyes, how many have green eyes?

The pie chart shows the favourite sauce of 32 people.

e) Which sauce is the least popular?

f) How many people like brown sauce?

g) How many people like BBQ sauce?

h) What fraction of the people like mayo?

The pie charts show men and women's favourite fruits.

i) What fraction of men liked cherries?

j) 12 males liked mangos, how many men were asked their preference?

k) Twice as many females were asked their preference than men. How many preferred pear?

l) How many more females preferred plums than men that preferred plums?

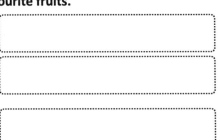

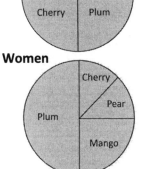

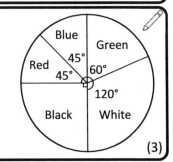

Exam question:

The pie chart shows the different colour socks worn by 30 football teams.

a) What fraction of the teams wear green socks?

b) How many teams don't wear white socks?

(3)

Pie charts with degrees

You will usually be given the degrees of each sector. To calculate the number of people in a sector, divide the total population by 360 (to get what 1° represents), then multiply by the number of degrees in the sector.

Example:

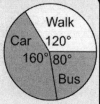

72 people were asked how they travel to school
Calculate the number of people represented by each sector

Car: 72 ÷ 360 x 160   = 32 people
Walk: 72 ÷ 360 x 120   = 24 people
Bus: 72 ÷ 360 x 80   = 16 people

You can check your answer by adding all of the sectors and seeing if you get back to the total

Practice questions:

The pie chart shows 90 peoples favourite colour.

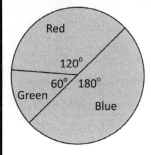

a) How many people liked blue?

b) How many people liked red?

c) How many more people liked blue than green?

The pie chart shows 288 peoples favourite sport.

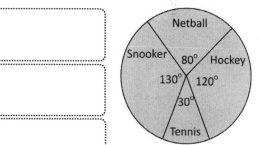

d) How many people chose snooker?

e) How many people chose tennis?

f) How many more people prefer hockey to netball?

The pie charts show data on 1728 people's sandwich preferences.

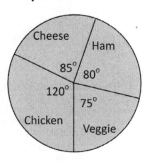

g) How many people like ham?

h) How many more people like Cheese than Veggie?

i) How many people prefer chicken or ham?

Exam question:

The pie chart shows the different meals ordered at a local public house on a lunchtime. 108 meals were ordered in total.

a) What fraction of the meals ordered were fish and chips?

b) How many burger meals were ordered?

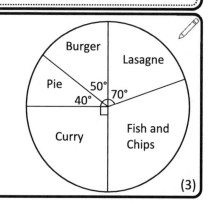

(3)

Drawing pie charts

When drawing pie charts, you need to calculate the angle for each sector.
To calculate the angles, sum the frequencies in your table to get the total Divide 360 by your total by to obtain the number of degrees that 1 value represents, then multiply it by the frequency of each sector.

Example:

The table shows data on peoples favourite colours.
Draw a pie chart to represent the data.

Colour	Frequency	Degrees
Blue	9	108
Red	2	24
Green	7	84
Pink	12	144
	30	

$360 \div 30 \times 9 = 108°$
$360 \div 30 \times 2 = 24°$
$360 \div 30 \times 7 = 84°$
$360 \div 30 \times 9 = 144°$

Draw a line from the centre to the top of the circle to start then measure the angles with a protractor.

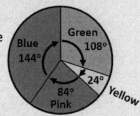

You can check your answers by adding all of the sectors and seeing if they total 360° – a full circle.

Practice questions:

Draw a pie charts to represent the following data:

a)

Fruit	Frequency
Apple	4
Banana	8
Plum	2
Mango	2

b)

Pet	Frequency
Dog	13
Cat	6
Rabbit	9
Snake	2

c)

Colour	Frequency
Orange	6
Yellow	4
Purple	7
Brown	3

Exam question:

Some children were asked to name their favourite flavour of ice cream. The table shows the results.

Draw an accurate pie chart to show the information in the table.

Flavour	Frequency
strawberry	15
vanilla	10
mint	20
chocolate	27

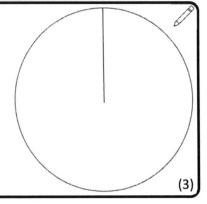

(3)

Probability scale

The probability of an event is an estimate of the likelihood or chance that it will happen. Probabilities can be described in words: **impossible** (the event cannot happen), **certain** (there is a 100% chance the event will happen), **even** (50% chance of an event happening), **unlikely** (less than 50% but not impossible), **likely** (more than 50% but not certain).

Examples

I roll a fair 6 sided dice, use a probability word to describe the probability I roll:

a) A seven → There is not a seven on the dice so it is **impossible**

b) An even number → There are 3 even numbers and three odd numbers on a dice: **Even chance**

c) A number less than 10 → All the numbers are less than 10: **Certain**

d) A number bigger than 1 → There are 5 numbers (out of 6) bigger than 1: **Likely**

Practice questions:

I spin a fair, 8 sided spinner as shown. Pick the correct word to match the event:

Impossible   Unlikely   Even   Likely   Certain

a) The spinner lands on A [　　　　]   b) The spinner lands on D [　　　　]

c) The spinner lands on a letter [　　　　]   d) The spinner lands on B [　　　　]

e) The spinner lands on an A or C [　　　　]   f) The spinner lands on C [　　　　]

In maths, probabilities are mostly given as a decimal between 0 and 1 or a fraction. A probability of 0 means an event is impossible and a probability of 1 means an event is certain.
A probability cannot be greater than 1.

Examples

I roll a fair 6 sided dice, On the number line mark the probability I roll:

a) A seven (A) → There is not a seven on the dice: **0**

b) An even number (B) → There are 3 even numbers and three odd numbers on a dice: **0.5**

c) A number less than 10 (C) → All the numbers are less than 10: **1**

d) A number bigger than 1 (D) → There are 5 numbers (out of 6) so mark 5 out of 6

Practice questions:

A bag contains 3 triangles, 2 circles and a square. A shape is picked at random.

On the probability scale mark (with a X) the probability I pick a:

g) Pentagon
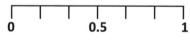

h) Triangle
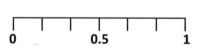

i) Triangle, circle or square
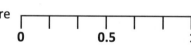

j) Circle
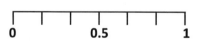

k) Black shape
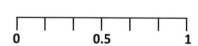

l) White shape

m) Square or circle
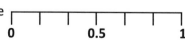

n) Square
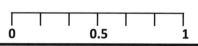

o) Black or grey shape
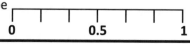

Probability

The probability of an event is a number between 0 and 1. A probability of 0 means the event is impossible and a probability of 1 means the event is certain to happen. When an event has a number of possibilities that are equally likely the following applies:

$$\text{Probability of an event} = \frac{\text{Number of times the event occurs}}{\text{Total number of possible outcomes}}$$

Examples

I roll a fair 6 sided dice, what is the probability I roll:

a) 3 → There is 1 three on a dice and there are 6 possibilities. **Probability** = $\frac{1}{6}$

b) An even number → There are 3 even numbers on a dice and there are 6 possibilities. **Probability** = $\frac{3}{6}$

c) A multiple of 3 → There are 2 multiples of 3 on a dice and there are 6 possibilities. **Probability** = $\frac{2}{6}$

Practice questions:

I roll a fair, 6 sided dice. Find the probability that I:

a) roll a 4.

b) roll a 6.

c) roll an odd number.

d) **don't** roll a 2.

e) roll a number less than 3.

f) roll a number over 6.

Practice questions:

I pick a random letter from the alphabet. Find the probability that I:

g) Pick a T.

h) Pick a Z.

i) Pick a vowel.

j) Pick a consonant.

k) Pick an A, B or C.

l) Pick a letter from the word MATHS.

Practice questions:

I pick a random number from the numbers 1 to 20. Find the probability that I:

m) Pick a multiple of 2.

n) Pick a number which is greater than 7.

o) Pick a number which is not a multiple of 3 or 5.

p) Pick a prime number.

q) **Don't** choose a square number.

r) Pick a triangular number.

s) Pick a factor of 24.

t) a multiple of 4 and a factor of 48.

Exam question:

A fair spinner has eight equal sections.
The sections are labelled 1, 2, 3, 4 and 5 as shown.
The spinner is spun.

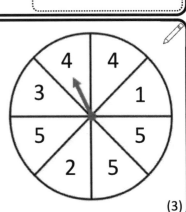

a) Which is the most likely letter that the arrow will land on?

b) What is the probability that the arrow lands on a 2?

c) What is the probability that the arrow lands on an odd number?

(3)

Relative frequency

The relative frequency is an estimate of the probability of an event. It is also called experimental probability You use the results of an experiment to estimate the probability. As you increase the number of trials in the experiment, the probability becomes more accurate.

$$\text{Relative frequency} = \frac{\text{Number of times the event occurs}}{\text{Number of trials}}$$

Examples

Tom rolls a biased dice 100 times and gets a four 7 times.

a) What is the relative frequency of getting a four? $\text{Relative frequency} = \frac{7}{100}$

He rolls the dice another 100 times and gets 3 more fours.

b) What is the new relative frequency? $\text{Relative frequency} = \frac{7+3}{100+100} = \frac{10}{200}$

Practice questions:

A coin is flipped 50 times, It lands on heads 13 times.

a) What is the relative frequency of flipping a head?

b) It is flipped another 50 times, and it lands on 17 more heads. What is the new relative frequency?

c) After a further 20 flips, it lands on tails 12 times. What is new relative frequency of getting a head?

Practice questions:

A biased dice is rolled 40 times, it lands on six 12 times.

d) What is the relative frequency of getting a six?

e) It is rolled another 60 times, and it lands on six 14 more times. What is the new relative frequency?

f) After another 160 rolls, it lands on six 46 times. What is new relative frequency of getting a six?

Practice questions:

Charlie is taking buttons out of a tub.
He takes out one button at a time at random, notes the colour, and replaces it in the tub

Red	Pink	Purple	Blue	Yellow
26	12	36	20	6

The table shows his results after 100 times

If Charlie takes out another button:

g) What is the relative frequency of him choosing blue or yellow?

h) What is the relative frequency of him choosing anything but purple?

Exam question:

A spinner has a green sector, blue sector and red sector.
The spinner is spun 300 times and it landed on red 124 times and on green 80 times.

a) What is the relative frequency of the spinner landing on blue?

b) From the next 100 spins, two fifths landed on green. What is the new relative frequency of the spinner landing on green?

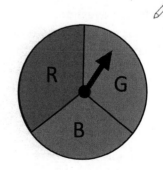

(3)

Expected Frequency

You can use the probability to estimate how many times an event should occur.
An estimate of the number of times an event will occur (**expected frequency**) = probability x number of trials.

Examples

a) Liz rolls a fair dice 300 times, estimate how many times she rolls a 3.

Probability of rolling a 3 = $\frac{1}{6}$, therefore expected frequency = $\frac{1}{6}$ x 300 = **50**

b) A factory tested 100 laptops and 3 were faulty, estimate how many faulty laptops there would be if they tested 840.

Relative frequency = $\frac{3}{100}$, therefore expected frequency = $\frac{3}{100}$ x 840 = 25.2 → to nearest laptop = **25**

Practice questions:

The probability of a mobile phone being faulty is $\frac{1}{20}$.

How many mobile phones would you expect to be faulty if you tested:

a) 100 phones?

b) 400 phones?

c) 2000 phones?

d) 832 phones?

Practice questions:

A coin is flipped 50 times of which 12 land on heads.

Estimate the number of heads you would expect if the coin was flipped;

e) 100 times.

f) 800 times.

g) 2000 times.

h) 240 times.

Practice questions:

Colin is counting different coloured cars on the motorway.
The table shows his results after 100 cars.

Red	Grey	Black	Blue	White
26	12	36	20	6

Estimate the number of **blue** cars he would see:

i) after 1000 cars.

j) after 850 cars.

k) after 240 cars.

l) after 190 cars.

Estimate the number of **grey** cars he would see:

m) after 500 cars.

n) after 350 cars.

o) after 240 cars.

p) after 585 cars.

Exam question:

A spinner has a green sector, blue sector and red sector.
The spinner is spun 300 times and it landed on red 141 times, and on green 102 times.

If it was spun another 200 times;

a) How many reds would you expect it to have landed on in **total**?

b) How many **more** times would you expect it to have landed on green than blue in 200 spins?

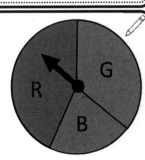

(3)

Sample spaces

A sample space is used to list all possible outcomes/possibilities of two combined events.

Example

A 6 sided dice is rolled and a spinner numbered 1 to 4 is spun
The scores are added together. Draw a sample space.

The outcomes for one event are listed along the top and the outcomes for the other event are listed down the side.

The combined outcomes are then filled in the middle.

The sample space shows the lowest and highest total and all the possibilities.

Dice

Spinner	1	2	3	4	5	6
1	2	3	4	5	6	7
2	3	4	5	6	7	8
3	4	5	6	7	8	9
4	5	6	7	8	9	10

Practice questions:

Complete the sample spaces:

a) Two spinners are numbered 1 to 4 and the scores are added.

	1	2	3	4
1				
2	3			
3			6	
4				

b) A fair six sided dice is rolled and a coin is flipped.

	1	2	3	4	5
H				H4	
T		T2			

c) A six sided dice and a spinner numbered 1 to 4. Their scores are multiplied.

	1	2	3	4	5	6
1						
2						
3						
4						

d) Two six sided dice are rolled and their scores are added.

	1	2	3	4	5	6
1						
2						
3						
4						
5						
6						

e) Spinner A is numbered 6, 3, 8, 7, 2, 9 and spinner B is numbered 4, 5, 6. The scores are multiplied.

	6	3	8	7	2	9
4						
5						
6						

f) Spinner A is numbered 4, 2, 7, 8, 3, 0 and spinner B is numbered 1 to 4. The score from B is subtracted from A.

	4	2	7	8	3	0
1						
2						
3						
4						

Exam question:

Two spinners are spun and the scores are multiplied together.
Complete the sample space to show all the possible results.

What is the **range** of the results?

Spinner A

Spinner B	3	4	5	6
1				
2				
3				
4				

(3)

Sample spaces can be used to calculate the probability of a combination of events.

Example

A 6 sided dice is rolled and a spinner numbered 1 to 4 is spun
The scores are added together.
Calculate the probability of:

a) Getting a total of 4.
   There are 3 ways of scoring four and
   there are <u>24 different outcomes</u>

$$\text{Probability} = \frac{3}{24}$$

a) Getting a total of more than 7.
   There are 6 ways of obtaining this.

$$\text{Probability} = \frac{6}{24}$$

Dice

Spinner		1	2	3	4	5	6
	1	2	3	4	5	6	7
	2	3	4	5	6	7	8
	3	4	5	6	7	8	9
	4	5	6	7	8	9	10

Practice questions:

Use the sample spaces to answer the questions.

What is the probability of:

	1	2	3	4
1	2	3	4	5
2	3	4	5	6
3	4	5	6	7
4	5	6	7	8

a) Scoring 5?

b) Scoring 8?

c) Scoring more than 6?

d) Scoring an even number?

What is the probability of:

	1	2	3	4	5	6
1	1	2	3	4	5	6
2	2	4	6	8	10	12
3	3	6	9	12	15	18
4	4	8	12	16	20	24

e) Scoring 7?

f) Scoring 4 or less?

g) Scoring an odd number?

h) Scoring a multiple of 3?

What is the probability of:

	6	3	8	7	2	9
4	24	12	32	28	8	36
5	30	15	40	35	10	45
6	36	18	48	42	12	54

i) Scoring a multiple of 5?

j) Scoring a factor of 48?

k) Scoring more than 20?

l) Scoring a square number?

Exam question:

Two spinners are spun and the numbers are multiplied.
All the possible results are shown in the sample space.

a) What is the probability that the result is **over** 15?

b) What is the probability that the result is an **odd** number?

Spinner A

Spinner B		6	3	7	2
	4	24	12	28	8
	5	30	15	35	10
	6	36	18	42	12

(2)

Combinations

You may be asked to list different combinations. This means you have to write down all the possible outcomes. It is best to work through methodically.

Example

Sandwiches are sold in either brown, white or seeded bread.
You can have cheese, ham or tuna sandwiches.
Write down the possible combinations of sandwiches.
It is often easy to abbreviate the words (Brown = B, White = W, etc)

Start with brown bread:	BC	BH	BT
Move onto white bread:	WC	WH	WT
Move onto seeded bread:	SC	SH	ST

There are **9 combinations** and this can be determined by the fact there were **3 x 3** options.

Practice questions:

a) For breakfast, Kira can eat cereal or toast and drink either orange or apple juice.
   Write down the possible combinations that Kira can have for breakfast.

b) Two pupils are picked from a class of boys and girls.
   Write down the possible combinations that could be chosen.

c) Paul can have either mint, strawberry or vanilla ice cream in a cone or a tub.
   Write down the possible combinations that Paul could have.

d) A restaurant serves pork, beef or lamb with either chips, roast potatoes or mash.
   Write down the possible combinations the restaurant serves.

e) Jack and Ken buy jacket potatoes. The potatoes come plain, with cheese of with beans.
   Write down the possible combinations of their 2 potatoes.

f) The letters ABCD can be written in a number of ways?
   Use the space below to list the combinations and state how many combinations there are.

   Number of combinations =

Exam question:

Here are four tiles. Each tile has a number on it.
They can be placed down in any order.
How many different **even** numbers can be made?

| 1 | 2 | 3 | 5 |

(2)

Solutions

Page 1:
a) Fifty b) Eight hundred c) Nine thousand d) Seventy thousand e) Three thousand
f) Five hundred thousand g) Three thousand h) Seven million i) Five tenths j) Eight tenths
k) Nine hundredths l) Eight hundredths m) One tenth n) Seven units o) Five thousandths
p) One hundredth

Exam question: a) Five hundred b) 86532 c) 86325

Page 2:
a) Four hundred and fifty two b) Eight hundred and thirty three
c) Nine thousand, one hundred and seventy four d) Seven thousand and sixty two
e) Twenty three thousand, nine hundred and forty f) Fifty six thousand, seven hundred and two
g) Six hundred and forty three thousand, five hundred and forty one
h) Seven million, four hundred and thirty two thousand, eight hundred and fifty two
i) 863 j) 29,218 k) 411,025 l) 6,014,212 m) 18,090,024

Exam question: a) Eighteen thousand, five hundred b) 7,117

Page 3:
a) 41, 34, 24, 14, 4 b) 762, 712, 612, 523, 62 c) 653, 432, 423, 334, 42 d) 531, 353, 341, 314
e) 2621, 2432, 2423, 258 f) 873, 871, 789, 781 g) 0.14, 0.4, 0.41, 1.4 h) 0.12, 0.23, 0.26, 0.76
i) 0.41, 1.14, 1.4, 4, 4.1 j) 0.0316, 0.04, 0.3, 0.315 k) 0.35, 0.351, 0.5, 0.531 l) 0.781, 8.71, 8.73, 78.9

Exam question: a) Snake, rabbit, parrot, cat, dog b) 15,559

Page 4:
a) 14, 5, -2, -4, -10 b) 12, 11, 9, -8, -10, -13 c) 53, 42, 6, 0, -34, -42 d) 14, 7, 1, -1, -9, -14
e) 42, -423, -432, -621 f) 790, 71, 18, -81, -789 g) -5, -4, -3, 2, 3 h) -17, -15, -12, 13, 14, 16
i) -41, -32, -8, 0, 24, 35 j) -19, -18, -4, -3, 4, 17 k) -432, -423, 5, 62, 421 l) -79, -71, -18, 16, 80

Exam question: a) Calgary, Moscow, Detroit, Leeds, Tokyo, Sydney b) 31°C

Page 5:
a) 135 b) 83 c) 731 d) 1221 e) 7751 f) 7272 g) 8.1 h) 17.32 i) 3.13 j) 91.43 k) 3.13 l) 104.31

Exam question: 13.3cm

Page 6:
a) 15 b) 219 c) 954 d) 863 e) 4794 f) 2463 g) 2.8 h) 5.7 i) 5.64 j) 62.29 k) 5.383 l) 75.543

Exam question: £3.49

Page 7:
a) 294 b) 1387 c) 4575 d) 4165 e) 6372 f) 14420 g) 4662 h) 10218

Exam question: £21.76

Page 8:
a) 1500 b) 500 c) 5.4 d) 105 e) 380 f) 3.7 g) 8.42 h) 38.05 i) 4.786 j) 9300 k) 520 l) 2100
m) 17800 n) 0.82 o) 9.04 p) 0.00124 q) 0.45 r) 0.00452

Exam question: a) 1080 b) 10^7 c) 420

Page 9:
a) 27 b) 62 c) 169 d) 21 e) 0.93 f) 2.27 g) 8.1 h) 0.69 i) 12.5 j) 264 k) 640 l) 1180 m) 92.4
n) 230.25 o) 492.4

Exam question: 397

Page 10:
a) 25 b) 3 c) 8 d) 98 e) 20 f) 32 g) 54 h) 4 i) $6 + 3 \times 5$ j) $6 \times 4 - 5 \times 3$ k) $5 \times (2 + 4)$ l) $(5 - 1) \times (6 + 4)$
m) $(2 + 6)^2 - 7$ n) $4 \times (5 + 4 \times 3)$

Exam question: Pat - You calculate powers before subtracting: $5 - 2^2 = 5 - 4 = 1$

Page 11:
a) Even b) Odd c) Odd d) Even e) Even f) Odd g) Even h) Even i) Odd j) No k) No l) No m) Yes
n) No o) No p) Yes q) No r) Yes

Exam question: Rational: 0.5   Prime: 5   Triangular: 21   Irrational: 5.73257524...

Page 12:
a) 3, 6, 9, 12, 15 b) 5, 10, 15, 20, 25 c) 11, 22, 33, 44, 55 d) 7, 14, 21, 28, 35 e) 15, 30, 45, 60, 75
f) 16, 32, 48, 64, 80 g) 25, 50, 75, 100, 125 h) 19, 38, 57, 76, 95 i) 27, 54, 81, 108, 135
j) 34, 68, 102, 136, 170 k) 62, 124, 186, 248, 310 l) 125, 250, 375, 500, 625
m) 15 n) 30 o) 14 p) 68 q) 30 r) 96 s) 60 t) 42 u) 110 v) 60

Exam question: 40 seconds

Page 13:
a) 1, 2, 3, 4, 6, 12 b) 1, 2, 4, 8, 16 c) 1, 3, 7, 21 d) 1, 3, 5, 15 e) 1, 2, 19, 38 f) 1, 7, 49 g) 1, 37
h) 1, 2, 5, 10, 25, 50 i) 1, 2, 3, 6, 13, 26, 39, 78 j) 1, 2, 3, 4, 6, 8, 12, 24 k) 1, 2, 4, 8, 16, 32, 64
l) 1, 2, 3, 4, 6, 7, 12, 14, 21, 28, 42, 84 m) 5 n) 7 o) 2 p) 4 q) 3 r) 30 s) 12 t) 12 u) 3 v) 9

Exam question: 4

Page 14:
a) 36 b) 16 c) 3 d) 1000 e) 49 f) 1 g) 81 h) 64 i) 2 j) 5 k) 10 l) 11 m) 10 n) 1 o) 5 p) 7

Exam question: a) 115 b) 5

Page 15:
a) 5, 9, 27 b) 10, 18, 20 c) 9 d) 27 e) 5, 10, 20 f) 9, 18, 27 g) 5 h) 10 i) 15, 17, 19, 21, 125 j) 16
k) 16 l) 125 m) 15, 21 n) 21 o) 17, 19 p) 15, 21 q) 1, 23 r) 6, 12, 36, 64, 78 s) 1, 36, 64 t) 1, 64
u) 1, 6, 12, 36 v) 78 w) 23 x) 1, 6, 36, 78

Exam question: a) 45 or 53 or 77 or 81 b) 56 or 70 or 77 c) 81

Page 16:

a)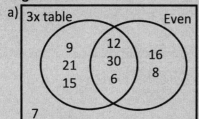

b)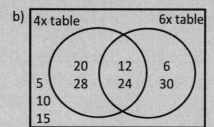

c)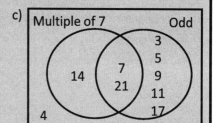

d)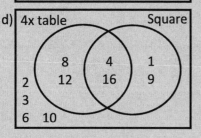

e)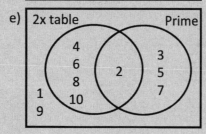

f)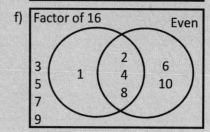

Page 16 continued:

g)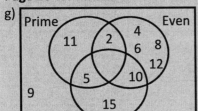

h)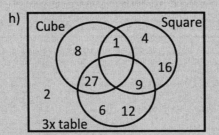

i)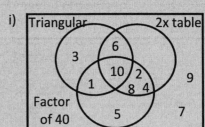

Exam question: a)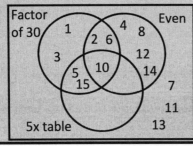

b) $\frac{3}{15}$

Page 17:

a) $\frac{1}{2}$ b) $\frac{1}{4}$ c) $\frac{1}{3}$ d) $\frac{3}{7}$ e) $\frac{2}{3}$ f) $\frac{2}{3}$ g) $\frac{2}{7}$ h) $\frac{7}{16}$ i) $\frac{2}{3}$ j) $\frac{3}{4}$ k) $\frac{3}{8}$ l) $\frac{1}{2}$ m) 20 n) 15 o) 21 p) 24 q) 8 r) 48 s) 90

t) 120 u) 9

Exam question: a) 2 b) 14

Page 18:

Set 1: a) $1\frac{3}{5}$ b) $3\frac{1}{3}$ c) $3\frac{2}{5}$ d) $5\frac{1}{4}$ e) $9\frac{1}{2}$ f) $3\frac{5}{6}$ g) $4\frac{1}{7}$ h) $6\frac{3}{5}$ i) $5\frac{7}{8}$ j) $15\frac{3}{4}$ k) $11\frac{7}{8}$ l) $27\frac{1}{3}$ m) $2\frac{7}{10}$

n) $13\frac{2}{5}$ o) $11\frac{5}{7}$ p) $15\frac{5}{6}$

Set 2: a) $\frac{9}{4}$ b) $\frac{11}{3}$ c) $\frac{13}{2}$ d) $\frac{23}{5}$ e) $\frac{23}{4}$ f) $\frac{37}{7}$ g) $\frac{53}{6}$ h) $\frac{39}{4}$ i) $\frac{55}{7}$ j) $\frac{47}{9}$ k) $\frac{79}{8}$ l) $\frac{60}{7}$ m) $\frac{48}{7}$ n) $\frac{51}{11}$ o) $\frac{41}{12}$ p) $\frac{51}{4}$

Exam question: a) $2\frac{1}{2}$ b) $6\frac{3}{4}$ c) $3\frac{2}{5}$

Page 19:

a) £6 b) £6 c) £24 d) £35 e) £16 f) £24 g) £35 h) £525

i) $\frac{7}{10}$ j) $\frac{4}{7}$ k) $\frac{1}{3}$ l) $\frac{8}{15}$ m) $\frac{3}{7}$ n) $\frac{1}{2}$ o) $\frac{7}{8}$ p) $\frac{2}{5}$ q) $\frac{4}{5}$ r) $\frac{4}{7}$ s) $\frac{11}{18}$ t) $\frac{2}{13}$ u) $\frac{2}{13}$ v) $\frac{9}{53}$ w) $\frac{1}{15}$

Exam question: $\frac{1}{4}$

Page 20:

a) 0.3 b) 0.45 c) 0.14 d) 0.125 e) 0.6 f) 0.34 g) 0.625 h) 0.25 i) 0.19

j) $\frac{1}{4}$ k) $\frac{27}{50}$ l) $\frac{11}{50}$ m) $\frac{17}{20}$ n) $\frac{18}{25}$ o) $\frac{19}{50}$ p) $\frac{1}{8}$ q) $\frac{33}{25}$ or $1\frac{8}{25}$

Exam question: $\frac{31}{250}$

Page 21:

a) 70% b) 35% c) 34% d) 37.5% e) 48% f) 45% g) 77.8% h) 41.7% i) 7.5%

j) $\frac{7}{20}$ k) $\frac{2}{5}$ l) $\frac{59}{100}$ m) $\frac{17}{20}$ n) $\frac{37}{50}$ o) $\frac{3}{8}$ p) $\frac{17}{40}$ q) $\frac{87}{1000}$

Exam question: $\frac{1}{16}$

Solutions

Page 31:
a) 0707 b) 0915 c) 2119 d) 0959 e) 1202 f) 3 g) 1116 h) 49 minutes i) 5 hours 12 minutes

Exam question: a) Priory Road b) 1202 or 12:02pm

Page 32:
a) £4.10 b) £5.70 c) £10.60 d) £18.20 e) £14.70 f) £10.80 g) £3.25 h) £6.85

Exam question: 47 hours

Page 33:
a) Formula b) Equation c) Expression d) Formula e) Identity f) Expression g) Expression h) Formula
i) Equation j) Formula k) Equation l) Identity m) Equation n) Formula

Exam question: A: Expression B: Formula C: Equation

Page 34:
a) $7x$ b) $3y$ c) $3x$ d) $5x$ e) $7c$ f) $13a$ g) $36a$ h) 0 i) $6x + 4y$ j) $7x + 7y$ k) $7x + 2y + 6$
l) $10x + 2y$ m) $11x + 4y$ n) $10x - 2y + 6$ o) $15a - 4b$ p) $8s + 2t + 6$ q) $7 + 2y - x$ r) $4x - 2y - 9$

Exam question: $5a + 4b$ and $2a + 2b$

Page 35:
a) $10xy$ b) $12ab$ c) $8xw$ d) $15uv$ e) $6t^2$ f) $8a^2$ g) $9a^2$ h) $10x^2y$ i) $24cd^2$ j) $6a^3$ k) $16a^2b^2$
l) $16a^3b^3$ m) $3a$ n) $20z$ o) $4x^2$ p) 20 q) $5a$ r) $4b$ s) $6t$ t) $\frac{1}{2}$ u) $\frac{1}{2a}$ v) $\frac{b}{3a}$ w) $\frac{3}{4a}$ x) $\frac{5}{7x}$

Exam question: $2ac$ and $2a$

Page 36:
a) $5x + 10$ b) $3a - 12$ c) $20 - 4y$ d) $32y - 24y$ e) $21x + 56$ f) $20a - 35$ g) $99 - 27y$ h) $y^2 - 3y$
i) $x^2 + 2x$ j) $6a^2 - 56a$ k) $12y^2 + 14y$ l) $8x - x^2$ m) $48x - 20x^2$ n) $12x + 30y$ o) $2a^2 + 16a$
p) $ab - 2a^2$ q) $a^3 - 2a^2$ r) $-4x - 20$ s) $-9x + 72$ t) $-3x^2 + 5x$ u) $-7y + 5y^2$ v) $6x^3 + 4x^2$
w) $2a^2b + 26ab$ x) $3a^2b^2 + 6a^3b$ y) $7xy^3 - 49x^2y$ z) $-5x^3y + 8x^4$

Exam question: $40x^3y - 32x^2y^2$

Page 37:
a) $x = 5$ b) $x = 15$ c) $x = 12$ d) $a = 6$ e) $a = 36$ f) $x = 10$ g) $x = -8$ h) $c = 2$ i) $a = -9$
j) $x = 10$ k) $x = 5$ l) $x = 10$ m) $x = 10$ n) $x = 18$ o) $x = -8$ p) $x = -6$ q) $x = -12$ r) $x = 6$

Exam question: $x = \frac{21}{6} = \frac{7}{2}$

Page 38:
a) x = 2 b) x = 5 c) x = 3 d) x = 4 e) x = 9 f) x = 7 g) x = 4 h) x = 6 i) x = 8 j) a = 11
k) t = 15 l) x = -1 m) c = -3 n) g = -2

Exam question: x = 3

Page 39:
a) x = 20 b) x = 2 c) x = 24 d) x = 84 e) x = 36 f) a = -32 g) h = 121 h) t = -26 i) x = 5 j) x = 19
k) x = 12 l) x = 26 m) a = 72 n) x = 6 o) s = 6 p) x = -22

Exam question: x = 24

Page 40:
a) $n + 5$ b) x - 4 c) $2x + 5$ d) $5b$ e) $0.8n$ f) $\frac{x}{2}$ g) $2(a + 5)$ h) $c^2 + 2$ i) $n + 5 = 12$ j) $n - 15 = 22$
k) $4x = 24$ l) $2x + 7 = 17$ m) $4a = 1.6$ n) $8x = 42$

Exam question: $12x = 36$, x = 3

Page 41:
a-h) Shown i) (5, 3) j) (-5, 5) k) (4, -3) l) (-4, 0)
m) (-8, 2) n) (6, 0) o) (0, 0) p) (-6, -9)

Exam question: Point shown, rectangle

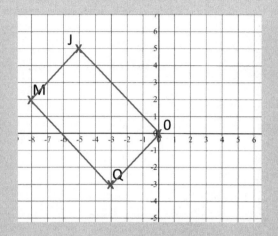

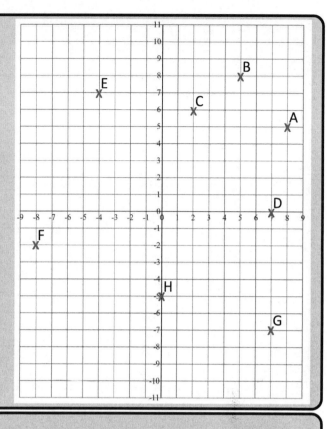

Page 42:
a) 15, 17, 19 b) 34, 38, 42 c) 12, 7, 2 d) 21, 28, 36 e) 23, 13, 2 f) 52, 70, 91 g) 0, -3, -6 h) 1, -4, -9
i) 224, 448, 896 j) 21, 34, 55 (Fibonacci) k) Add 3 l) Subtract 6 m) Add 11 n) Add 1 then 2 then 3...
o) Add 5 times table p) Divide by 2 q) Subtract 7 then 6 then 5... r) Square numbers s) Subtract 7
t) Subtract the two terms before

Exam question: 14, 17

Page 43:
a) False b) True c) True d) True e) True f) False g) False h) True i) False j) True k) True l) False
m) 6, 5, 4, 3, 2 n) 4, 5, 6, 7, 8 o) 13, 14, 15, 16, 17 p) 15, 14, 13, 12, 11 q) 7, 8, 9, 10, 11 r) 2, 1, 0, -1, -2
s) 11, 10, 9, 8, 7 t) 21, 22, 23, 24, 25 u) 3, 4, 5, 6 v) 7, 8, 9 w) 0, 1, 2, 3, 4, 5 x) 8, 9, 10, 11, 12
y) -1, 0, 1, 2, 3, 4 z) 7 α) -5, -4, -3, -2, -1, 0, 1 β) 5

Page 44:
a) 4cm b) 8.5cm c) 5.7cm d) 7.4cm e) 4.9cm f) 5.6cm g) 6.6cm

Exam question: a) 7.1cm b) 3.4cm

Page 45:
a) Acute b) Right angle c) Obtuse d) Acute e) Straight line f) Reflex g) Acute h) Reflex i) Acute
j) Acute k) Obtuse l) Acute m) Obtuse n) Reflex o) Right angle p) Obtuse q) Acute r) Obtuse
s) Obtuse t) Reflex u) Reflex v) Straight line w) Reflex

Exam question: Acute

Page 46:
a) 80° b) 55° c) 35° d) 115° e) 105° f) 120°

Exam question: a) $x = 135°$ b) $y = 225°$

Page 47: Angles drawn

Page 48: triangles drawn – check with ruler and protractor

Page 49: Triangles drawn – check with ruler

Page 50:
a) Equilateral b) Scalene c) Isosceles d) Right e) Scalene f) Right / Scalene g) Isosceles h) Scalene
i) Scalene j) Isosceles k) Equilateral l) Scalene m) Isosceles n) Isosceles o) Isosceles p) Scalene / Right

Exam question: 50° and 80° or 65° and 65°

Page 51:
a) Rectangle b) Rhombus c) Trapezium d) Kite e) Parallelogram f) Square g) Rhombus h) Trapezium
i) Square j) Rectangle k) Kite l) Parallelogram

Exam question: a) Square and rhombus b) Parallelogram and rhombus

Page 52:
a) 50° b) 55° c) 63° d) 41° e) 35° f) 31° g) 51.5° h) 29.4° i) 120° j) 65° k) 55° l) 40°
m) 39° n) 60° o) 88° p) 9°

Exam question: 57°

Page 53:
a) 220° b) 245° c) 198° d) 113° e) 140° f) 140° g) 80° h) 73° i) No – 190° j) No – 179° k) No - 179°
l) Yes - 180°

Exam question: Angle EBC = 180 – 30 – 90 = 60°, Angle DEB = 180 – 30 – 30 = 120°,
Angle BEC = 180 – 120 = 60°, Angle BCE = 60° so BEC is an equilateral triangle.

Page 54:
a) 30° b) 50° c) 55° d) 50° e) 60° f) 25° g) 126° h) 47° i) 60° j) 22.6° k) 45.6° l) 34°

Exam question: 30°

Page 55:
a) 110° b) 80° c) 120° d) 70° e) 45° f) 54° g) 112° h) 226° i) 112.5° j) 123° k) 31.8° l) 81°

Exam question: 60°

Page 56:
a) E and G b) C and E c) B, D and F d) E e) B, C and D f) D and F

Exam question: 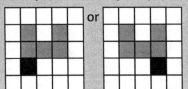 or and

Page 57:
a) 1 b) 1 c) 2 d) 1 e) 1 f) 0 g) 0 h) 6 i) 4 j) 3
k)   l)   m)   n)

o) 2 p) 1 q) 2 r) 3

Exam question: a)   or   or   b)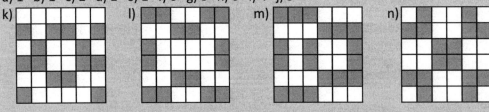

Page 58:

a) 2 b) 2 c) 2 d) 4 e) 2 f) 1 g) 6 h) 4 i) 1 j) 3

k) 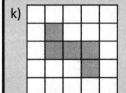 l) 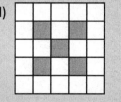 m) 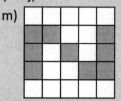 n)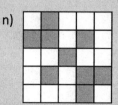

Exam question: a) 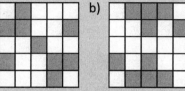 b)

Page 59:

a) 7 b) 34 c) 27 d) 5.4 e) 17.5 f) 3.25 g) 5.2 h) 32.2 i) 8.95 j) 9.7

Exam question: 3.8

Page 60:

a) 8cm b) 8cm c) 12cm d) 12cm e) 10cm f) 16cm g) 12cm h) 16cm i) 12cm j) 18cm k) 45cm
l) 34cm m) 56m n) 68mm

Exam question: 14 ÷ 4 = 3.5 so can't be drawn.

Page 61:

a) 28mm b) 147cm c) 142m d) 76cm e) 189cm f) 240mm g) 36cm h) 38cm i) 96cm j) 334m
k) 192cm l) 258m

Exam question: 76cm

Page 62:

a) $3cm^2$ b) $4cm^2$ c) $8cm^2$ d) $5cm^2$ e) $16cm^2$ f) $12cm^2$ g) $16cm^2$ h) $2cm^2$ i) $4.5cm^2$ j) $8cm^2$ k) $4cm^2$
l) $8cm^2$ m) $24.5cm^2$ n) $4cm^2$ o) $16.5cm^2$ p) $5cm^2$ q) $22.5cm^2$ r) $12cm^2$ s) $6cm^2$

Exam question: $36cm^2$

Page 63:

a) $12cm^2$ b) $32cm^2$ c) $28cm^2$ d) $39m^2$ e) $121cm^2$ f) $90m^2$ g) 4cm h) 8cm i) 11mm j) 10cm k) 6cm
l) 5cm

Exam question: 4cm

Page 64:

a) $6cm^2$ b) $12cm^2$ c) $12cm^2$ d) $24cm^2$ e) $42cm^2$ f) $12.5m^2$ g) 10cm h) 4cm i) 10cm j) 6m k) 4cm
l) 8cm

Exam question: $50cm^2$

Page 65:

a) $24cm^2$ b) $9cm^2$ c) $77cm^2$ d) $35cm^2$ e) $54cm^2$ f) $132cm^2$ g) 4cm h) 7cm i) 6.5cm j) 10.5cm
k) 5.2m l) 2.5cm

Exam question: 4.5cm

Page 66:

a) $32cm^2$ b) $18cm^2$ c) $30cm^2$ d) $24cm^2$ e) $75cm^2$ f) $66m^2$ g) 7cm h) 5.5cm i) 4cm j) 7cm
k) 3m l) 4.5mm

Exam question: $36m^2$

Page 67:
a) 43cm² b) 51cm² c) 41cm² d) 114m² e) 60mm² f) 60m² g) 211m² h) 141cm² i) 353cm²

Exam question: 18m²

Page 68:
a) 30cm² b) 102.5cm² c) 36cm² d) 78cm² e) 108m² f) 108mm² g) 58.5cm² h) 63m²

Exam question: 32m²

Page 69:
a) Parallel b) Perpendicular c) Neither d) Neither e) Parallel f) Parallel g) Perpendicular h) Neither
i) FG j) CD k) YZ and UV l) VW, UZ and XY m) QT n) OR o) YZ p) VZ

q) 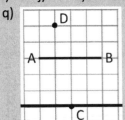 r) 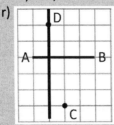 s) 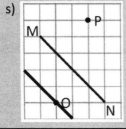 t)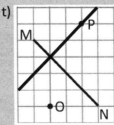

Page 70:
a) Diameter b) Radius c) Circumference d) Chord e) Arc f) Chord g) Tangent h) Sector i) Sector
j) Segment k) Sector l) Segment

Exam question: a) Diameter b) Chord c) Radius

Page 71:
a) Name: Pyramid Faces: 5 Vertices: 5 Edges: 8 b) Name: Cube Faces: 6 Vertices: 8 Edges: 12
c) Name: Triangular prism Faces: 5 Vertices: 6 Edges: 9
d) Name: Cuboid Faces: 6 Vertices: 8 Edges: 12 e) Name: Sphere Faces: 1 Vertices: 0 Edges: 0
f) Name: Cylinder Faces: 3 Vertices: 0 Edges: 2 g) Name: Cone Faces: 2 Vertices: 1 Edges: 1

Page 72:
a) 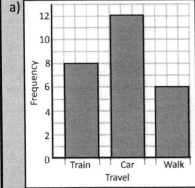 b) 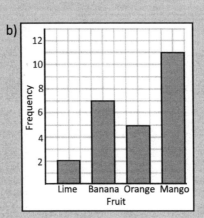 c)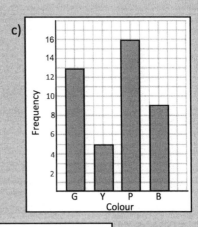

d)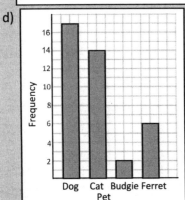

Exam question: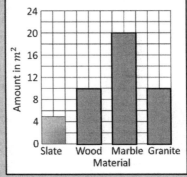

Page 73:

a) 4   b) 24   c) 8   d) 7   e) 31   f) 1   g) 22   h) 108   i) 12   j) 17   k) Wednesday   l) 14

Exam question: a) 21   b) 5

Page 74:

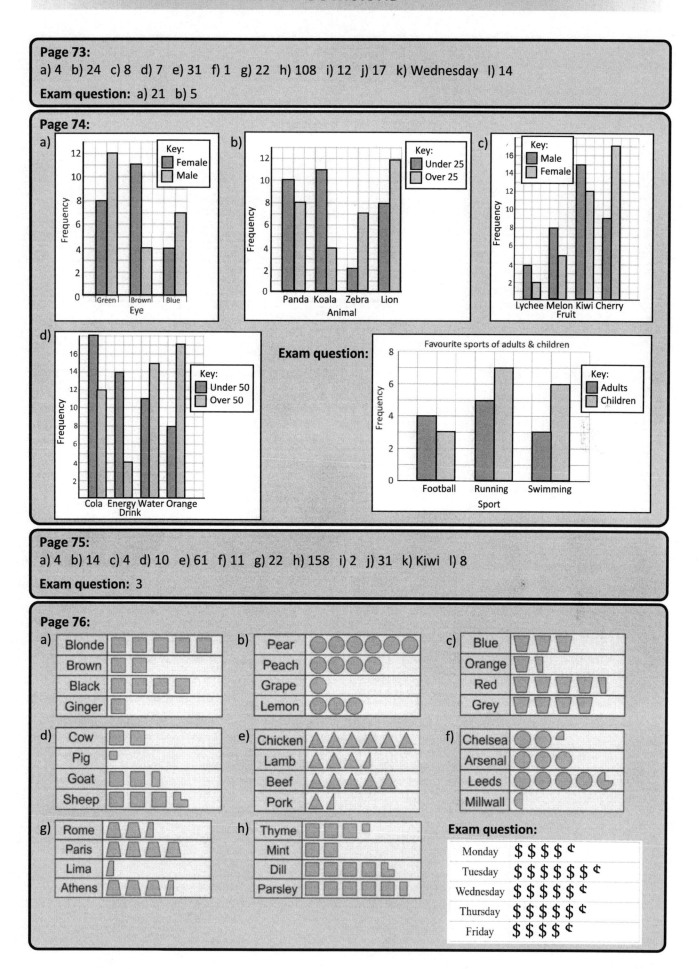

Page 75:

a) 4   b) 14   c) 4   d) 10   e) 61   f) 11   g) 22   h) 158   i) 2   j) 31   k) Kiwi   l) 8

Exam question: 3

Page 76:

Page 77:

a) 6 b) 12 c) 42 d) 15 e) 14 f) 9 g) 34 h) 5 i) 48 j) 22 k) 116 l) 22

Exam question: a) 2 strikes b) 3

Page 78:

a) Brown : 12, Black : 3, Blonde : 9, Other : 6 b) 5 : 15, 6 : 11, 7 : 0, 8 : 4

c) Green : ₪₪ || (7) , Blue : ₪₪ ||| (8) , Brown : ₪₪ ₪₪ ₪₪ (15)

d) 0 : ₪₪ ₪₪ | (11) , 1 : ₪₪ ₪₪ ₪₪ ||| (18) , 2 : ₪₪ ₪₪ ₪₪ (15) , 3 : ₪₪ ₪₪ (10) , 4 : ||| (3) ,
5 : ||| (3)

Exam question: 2 : | (1) , 3 : | (1) , 4 : |||| (4) , 5: ₪₪ | (6) , 6 : ||| (3) , 7 : |||| (4) , 8 : || (2)

Page 79:

a) Frequencies: 3, 7, 11, 7 b) Frequencies: 4, 7, 5, 4, 6, 4 c) Frequencies: 4, 1, 7, 5, 4, 3

Exam question: Frequencies: 1, 12, 2, 1

Page 80:

a) 9 b) 15 c) 7 d) 5 e) 25 f) 4.8 g) 5 h) 7 i) 4 j) 6.5 k) 5.4 l) 3.5

Exam question: 3.5

Page 81:

a) 8 b) 12 c) 7 d) 6 e) 13 f) 3 and 5 g) 1 and 2 h) 12 i) No mode j) 2 k) No mode l) -13
m) 18 n) 13 o) 11 p) 11 q) 43 r) 16 s) 35 t) 11 u) 15 v) 62

Exam question: a) 6 b) 5

Page 82:

a) 5 b) 5 c) 6 d) 8 e) 8 f) 36.2 g) 52.857... h) 60.166... i) 7.65 j) 6.56 k) 2.2 l) -4.333...
m) 15°C n) 31°C

Exam question: No, mean of the girls is 43 seconds which is faster than the boys mean.

Page 83:

a) 15 b) 14 c) 23 d) 22 e) 44 f) 6 g) 14 h) 19 i) 71 j) 18 k) 23 l) 62 m) 56 n) 212

Exam question: a) 161 b) 13

Page 84:

a)

9	8	17
9	4	13
18	12	30

b)

14	13	27
18	6	24
32	19	51

c)

14	7	6	27
3	8	12	23
17	15	18	50

d)

18	18	27	63
18	23	15	56
36	41	42	119

e)

11	13	24
12	14	26
23	27	50

f)

25	7	12	44
21	11	4	36
46	18	16	80

Exam question: a)

16	13	16	45
12	19	18	49
28	32	34	94

b) 28

Page 85:

a) $\frac{7}{20}$ b) $\frac{9}{20}$ c) $\frac{6}{11}$ d) $\frac{21}{50}$ e) $\frac{8}{50}$ f) $\frac{11}{24}$ g) $\frac{35}{100}$ h) $\frac{66}{100}$ i) $\frac{14}{34}$

Exam question: a) $\frac{46}{150}$ b) $\frac{3}{53}$

Page 86:

a) Brown b) Green c) 10 d) 4 e) BBQ and mayo f) 8 g) 4 h) $\frac{1}{8}$ i) $\frac{1}{4}$ j) 24 k) 6 l) 18

Exam question: a) $\frac{60}{360} = \frac{1}{6}$ b) 20

Page 87:

a) 45 b) 30 c) 30 d) 104 e) 24 f) 32 g) 384 h) 48 i) 960

Exam question: a) $\frac{110}{360} = \frac{11}{36}$ b) 15

Page 88:

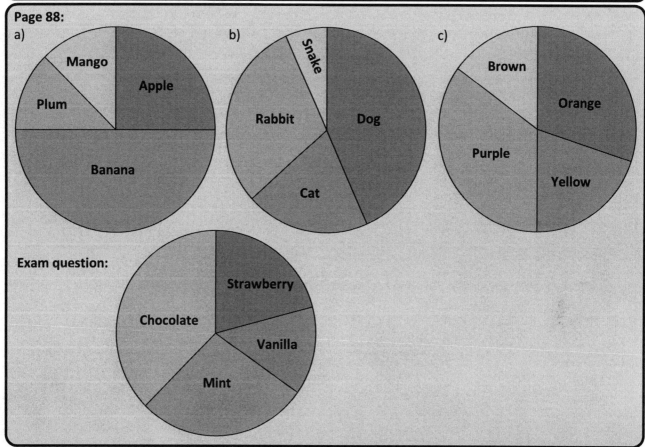

a) Mango, Apple, Plum, Banana

b) Snake, Rabbit, Dog, Cat

c) Brown, Orange, Purple, Yellow

Exam question:

Strawberry, Chocolate, Vanilla, Mint

Page 89:

a) Even b) Impossible c) Certain d) Unlikely e) Likely f) Unlikely g)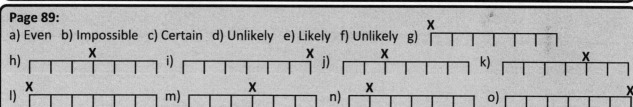

h)   i)   j)   k)

l)   m)   n)   o)

Page 90:

a) $\frac{1}{6}$ b) $\frac{1}{6}$ c) $\frac{3}{6}$ d) $\frac{5}{6}$ e) $\frac{2}{6}$ f) 0 g) $\frac{1}{26}$ h) $\frac{1}{26}$ i) $\frac{5}{26}$ j) $\frac{21}{26}$ k) $\frac{3}{26}$ l) $\frac{5}{26}$ m) $\frac{10}{20}$ n) $\frac{13}{20}$ o) $\frac{11}{20}$ p) $\frac{8}{20}$ q) $\frac{16}{20}$ r) $\frac{5}{20}$

s) $\frac{7}{20}$ t) $\frac{4}{20}$

Exam question: a) 5 b) $\frac{1}{8}$ c) $\frac{5}{8}$

Page 91:

a) $\frac{13}{50}$ b) $\frac{30}{100}$ c) $\frac{38}{120}$ d) $\frac{12}{40}$ e) $\frac{26}{100}$ f) $\frac{72}{260}$ g) $\frac{26}{100}$ h) $\frac{64}{100}$

Exam question: a) $\frac{96}{300}$ b) $\frac{120}{400}$

Page 92:

a) 5 b) 20 c) 100 d) 41.6 or 42 e) 24 f) 192 g) 480 h) 57.6 or 58 i) 200 j) 170 k) 48 l) 38 m) 60
n) 42 o) 28.8 or 29 p) 70.2 or 70

Exam question: a) 235 b) 30

Solutions

Page 93:

a)

2	3	4	5
3	4	5	6
4	5	6	7
5	6	7	8

b)

H1	H2	H3	H4	H5
T1	T2	T3	T4	T5

c)

1	2	3	4	5	6
2	4	6	8	10	12
3	6	9	12	15	18
4	8	12	16	20	24

d)

2	3	4	5	6	7
3	4	5	6	7	8
4	5	6	7	8	9
5	6	7	8	9	10
6	7	8	9	10	11
7	8	9	10	11	12

e)

24	12	32	28	8	36
30	15	40	35	10	45
36	18	48	42	12	54

f)

3	1	6	7	2	-1
2	0	5	6	1	-2
1	-1	4	5	0	-3
0	-2	3	4	-1	-4

Exam question: Range = 21

Page 94:

a) $\frac{4}{16}$ b) $\frac{1}{16}$ c) $\frac{3}{16}$ d) $\frac{8}{16}$ e) 0 f) $\frac{8}{24}$ g) $\frac{6}{24}$ h) $\frac{12}{24}$ i) $\frac{6}{18}$ j) $\frac{5}{18}$ k) $\frac{12}{18}$ l) $\frac{2}{18}$

Exam question: a) $\frac{7}{12}$ b) $\frac{2}{12}$

Page 95:

a) CO CA TO TA b) BB BG GB GG c) MC MT SC ST VC VT d) PC PR PM BC BR BM LC LR LM
e) PP PC PB CP CC CB BP BC BB f) 24 combinations (ABCD, ABDC, ACBD, ACDB, ADBC, ADCB, BACD, BADC, BCAD, BCDA, BDAC, BDCA, CABD, CADB, CBAD, CBDA, CDAB, CDBA, DABC, DACB, DBAC, DBCA, DCAB, DCBA)

Exam question: 6

108

Printed in Great Britain
by Amazon

40576626R00064